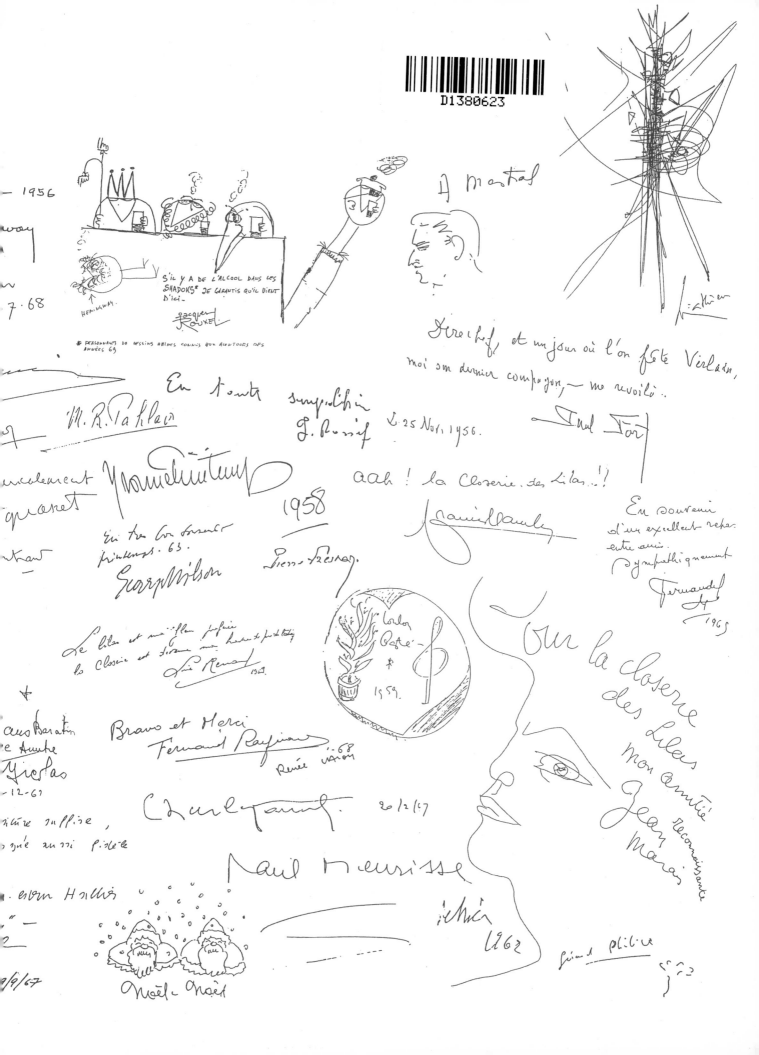

Cafés d'Artistes à Paris

...hier et aujourd'hui

Textes Gérard-Georges Lemaire
Photos Martin H. M. Schreiber

ÉDITIONS PLUME

L'éditeur remercie les personnes suivantes pour leur aide précieuse et leur collaboration :

Sylvie Buisson et Christian Parisot,
Archive Photos,
Nathalie Borot,
Olivier Corpet, IMEC,
Catherine Aygalinc,
Madame Carole Siljejovic du Café de Flore et de la Closerie des Lilas,
Monsieur Perrochon de la Brasserie Lipp,
Madame Mathivat des Deux Magots,
Madame Nadine Groc de la Coupole,
Monsieur Mazière du Sélect,
Monsieur Robert du Dôme,
Monsieur Mathieu du Lapin Agile,
Monsieur Gille du Moulin de la Galette.

Direction d'ouvrage
Catherine Laulhère-Vigneau

Conception graphique
Anne Flemming, Anne-Laure Descombins

Coordination éditoriale
Emmanuelle Laudon

Photogravure
Delta +, Paris

Éditions Plume
2, rue de la Roquette, 75011 Paris

OUVRAGE RÉALISÉ AVEC LE CONCOURS DE

Café de Colombia

"Un Américain à Paris"

Café ! Y a-t-il mot plus magique, plus riche d'images évoquées, plus intemporel, surtout quand on le prononce à New York ! À Manhattan, des lois mystérieuses réglementent l'espace et l'occupation des trottoirs et interdisent à un restaurant ou à un débit de boissons de s'étendre en extérieur. Dans les années 80, quelques audacieux ont planté leurs tables, leurs chaises et quelques parasols devant leur façade, et ont affronté les instances locales pour acquérir ce droit et ce privilège. Les tentatives sont restées bien rares, rien à voir avec le charme de Paris, la capitale des Cafés.

À Paris depuis juin 1989, j'ai d'abord vécu dans le VIᵉ arrondissement et je suis devenu un fidèle client du Flore, des Deux Magots, de Lipp et de La Palette. Ces cafés m'ont tout de suite fasciné par leur atmosphère, leurs caractères. J'ai appris à reconnaître les habitués qui, jour après jour, choisissaient le même emplacement ou retrouvaient le même groupe d'amis ou noircissaient du papier, d'un air pénétré de leur importance, sans cesser de jeter des coups d'œil alentour, pour vérifier qu'on les remarquait. Sans oublier les garçons, les directeurs, le flot constant de visiteurs des quatre coins du monde, avec leurs habitudes et leurs signes distinctifs collectifs et personnels.

Chaque café a son propre rythme, sa vie spécifique, bien différents du café voisin même si les deux se touchent littéralement. Mais ils ont un point commun très fort. Ils font partie intégrante de la vie de leurs clients et de la ville elle-même. Le café est l'extension du lieu de travail ou du domicile, le lieu où l'on rencontre ou reçoit comme dans son salon (en mieux !), où l'on se détend en lisant tranquillement son journal ou le dernier roman acheté. Mais quel délice aussi de rêvasser toute la journée devant la même tasse de café sans se sentir obligé de partir ou de commander autre chose. Les premiers temps, je me rappelle, je choisissais systématiquement le même coin ensoleillé d'un café pour voir défiler les autres consommateurs. Il m'est arrivé de piquer un somme et de m'éveiller l'ombre venue, avec un entourage complètement renouvelé. Jamais un serveur ne m'a réveillé pour que je commande autre chose. Unique, je vous dis !

Et voilà d'où viennent les photos de cafés que vous allez voir. Il n'y a pas si longtemps, on tolérait les appareils photo sans problème. C'était avant certains incidents désagréables ou quelques négligences de photo-journalistes, qui, en changeant la perception du public, ont contribué à nous rendre la vie plus difficile, parfois. Je ne peux plus photographier spontanément une scène belle ou charmante, s'il y a quelqu'un dans le champ. Cartier-Bresson, Robert Doisneau, André Kertesz, Brassaï et autres font partie d'un temps révolu. L'époque n'est plus à l'innocence ou à la tolérance, c'est celle des modèles déposés et des droits d'auteur... Aujourd'hui il est impossible de prendre une photo d'un inconnu sans que cela devienne une opération à organiser. Et c'est bien triste. Voilà pourquoi certaines des photographies présentées sont un peu des natures mortes. Car, après tout, qu'est-ce qu'un café sans ceux qui le fréquentent. Des chaises, des tables, des murs ou une décoration ne font pas un café, il manque les êtres humains qui l'animent, les clients, les serveurs, les tenanciers, les touristes et les artistes des rues, c'est-à-dire le cœur et l'âme de ces cafés.

Alors, si, un jour, du coin de l'œil, vous voyez quelqu'un viser dans votre direction, ne vous alarmez ni ne vous énervez pas, je vous en prie ! Vous ne ferez pas demain la couverture de *Paris Match* ou de *Time magazine*. D'ailleurs, ce n'est peut-être même pas vous dans l'objectif, mais la tasse sur votre table, la lumière sur les chaises au passage du serveur, ou n'importe quoi, absolument sans lien avec vous. Faites comme si de rien n'était et permettez à cette personne d'être créatrice et, peut-être, de capturer une vision magique et intemporelle, au lieu de lui jeter un regard assassin, ou de l'empêcher de prendre la photo le gênant avec un journal ou votre main. Ce serait du temps et du travail gâché, dommage. La plupart du temps, personne n'a l'intention de profiter de vous, sauf si vous êtes une star, un politicien ou un V.I.P. Alors, souriez, détendez-vous et soyez heureux en une fraction de seconde d'être un cadeau au présent et au futur.

Choisissez un café, passez-y plusieurs heures, revenez les jours suivants à la même heure : petit à petit vous entrerez dans la magie de son théâtre.

Merci à tous ceux qui ont toléré ma présence, bien que, peut-être, j'ai troublé leur calme. Qu'ils sachent que ma seule intention, toujours, était de fixer un moment intemporel. Merci à tous, et surtout aux "garçons" qui m'ont laissé assis des heures face à un verre d'eau ; et aussi à tous les directeurs de ces cafés, bien sûr, pour leur compréhension et leur coopération.

Je remercie particulièrement Jacques Mathivat et Catherine Mathivat, Francis Dupin, Thierry Cuzuel et Michel... du Café Les Deux Magots pour leur gentillesse et leur générosité. M. Siljejovic, Francis Boussard, Daniel Dennielou et Jean... du Café de Flore.
Et également la Brasserie Lipp, La Closerie des Lilas, Le Sélect, Le Dôme et La Coupole.

Martin H.M. Schreiber

S O M M

A I R E

Montmartre

Montparnasse

Saint-Germain-des-Prés

C. Grolleau

Montmartre

8

HIER...

Au XIXᵉ siècle, Paris connaît une expansion extraordinaire. De vieux quartiers disparaissent et de nouveaux surgissent du néant. De grands travaux d'urbanisme sont entrepris au nord, à commencer par la Nouvelle Athènes. C'est là, en dessous de la barrière de Pigalle, que l'univers romantique élit domicile. De grands tragédiens, comme Talma, Mlle Mars ou Duchesnois y font construire leur hôtel particulier. La Malibran s'installe impasse de l'Élysée-des-Beaux-Arts. George Sand et Frédéric Chopin y abritent quelque temps leurs amours tempétueuses. C'est aussi dans ces rues où cohabitent bourgeois et artistes, que s'épanouit le commerce galant de ces jeunes hétaïres qu'on surnomme les " lorettes ".

Montmartre est encore à cette époque une commune bucolique protégée des agitations de la ville. Les citadins en fréquentent les abords immédiats à la recherche de plaisirs simples. Plusieurs guinguettes et bals populaires existent déjà à l'aube du siècle dernier, comme le Bal du Grand Turc, rue des Poissonniers où la colonie allemande aime à se retrouver dès 1806. De tous ces endroits, *L'Élysée-Montmartre*, édifié sur l'ancienne chaussée de Rochechouart, ouvert vers 1807, est celui qui connaît le plus grand succès. C'est un bal tout à fait respectable, fréquenté par de bons bourgeois désireux de s'encanailler à la belle saison et d'où sont chassées les personnes de "mauvaise mine".

Bientôt Montmartre compte plusieurs établissements réservés à la musique et à la danse, comme le Bal de la Boule-Blanche, créé en 1822 à la place de la Belle en Cuisses, qu'on rebaptise plus tard le Bal de la Boule-Noire tant il est devenu sale, ou les Folies Robert, inaugurées en 1856, qui donnent sur l'impasse du Cadran.

Pages précédentes :
Les moulins de Montmartre en 1843. À l'époque Montmartre est encore un paisible village avec ses vignobles, ses cultures maraîchères et ses moulins.

Page de gauche :
Au Moulin-Rouge par P. Massé. Le succès retentissant de ce nouveau genre de café-concert établit définitivement la gloire de Montmartre.

Ci-dessus : **Une rue de Montmartre au début du siècle.**

Au cours du XIXe siècle, Montmartre se transforme rapidement en un des pôles des plaisirs des Parisiens qui viennent s'encanailler dans les grands bals de la Butte.

Ci-dessus : L'Élysée-Montmartre reste longtemps le prince des bals où le bourgeois côtoie l'apache, le mauvais garçon de la zone.

Ci-contre : La Mairie de Montmartre sur la place du Tertre.

LE VIEUX MONTMARTRE

D'une certaine manière, c'est Henri Murger qui invente la vie de bohème dans cette région encore vierge de la cité puisqu'il lance la *Brasserie des Martyrs* gérée par les frères Schœn. Très vite, cette maison où l'on "boit à l'allemande" attire l'intelligentsia : Charles Baudelaire, le peintre François Bonvin, l'écrivain Edmond Duranty, le directeur de la revue *Réalisme*, le critique Champfleury, Castagnary, tous des proches et des émules de Gustave Courbet, qui y règne en maître incontesté et y diffuse ses idées sur l'art et la politique. En fin d'après-midi, le photographe et écrivain Nadar, l'éditeur Poulet-Malassis, le jeune avocat Léon Gambetta aiment à se plonger dans cette atsmophère saturée de tabac et d'effluves de bière. Édouard Manet, qui a abandonné le très élégant

perron du Café Tortoni sur le boulevard des Italiens, ne craint pas de pénétrer dans cette antre de rebelles en train de préparer des révolutions ou d'élaborer des utopies. Ce grand laboratoire des idées encore virtuelles connaît une seconde génération d'habitués, regroupés pour l'essentiel autour de Xavier de Ricard, le fondateur de la *Revue du progrès moral, littéraire, scientifique et artistique*. Alphonse Daudet, Gustave Kahn évoluent au milieu de cette faune de lettrés et de journalistes, de peintres et de graveurs de notoriétés diverses et variées que les frères Goncourt exècrent plus que tout.

Le très discret *Café Guerbois*, situé Grande-Rue-des-Batignolles, presque parois-

sial, peuplé exclusivement de rentiers et de retraités, possède une salle dans une crypte à plafond bas offrant, au milieu des années 1860, un cadre aux réunions d'un cercle d'artistes et d'écrivains dont l'incontestable fédérateur est Manet dont l'atelier est proche. Il y a là Émile Zola et Duranty, les graveurs Belloc et Desboutin, Zacharie Astruc, Constantin Guys, Nadar, le paysagiste Guillemet, l'orientaliste Tobar, le collectionneur et critique Théodore Duret, puis Auguste Renoir, Claude Monet et Camille Pissarro. Les débats qui s'y déroulent finissent par formuler les grands axes théoriques de ce qui sera appelé plus tard l'impressionnisme. On ne parle encore que d'École des Batignolles, que Fantin-Latour immortalise dans une célèbre composition exécutée en 1870. Ce cercle ne cesse de s'élargir au fil des ans. Le Méridional Frédéric Bazille s'associe aux causeries du jeudi après-midi, tout comme l'écrivain Armand Sylvestre. Les discussions ne sont pas toujours sereines : en 1870 Manet et Duranty se disputent à tel point qu'ils

Le Petit Journal

LE VIEUX PARIS S'EN VA

Ci-dessus : La Brasserie des Martyrs, située à deux pas de la place Pigalle, est un véritable chaudron de sorcières. On y agite les idées les plus radicales et les adeptes du réalisme y tiennent le haut du pavé.

Ci-contre : La démolition des derniers moulins de Montmartre en 1911. Victime de sa gloire et de l'urbanisation, Montmartre est presque entièrement défigurée à la veille de la Grande Guerre.

Les artistes, désormais habitués des cafés, en font un de leurs thèmes favoris dans l'optique de la représentation de la vie moderne.

Ci-dessus : Claude Monet vu par Renoir.

Ci-contre :
Edgar Degas, *Au café* ou *L'Absinthe* peint vers 1875/1876 (musée d'Orsay, Paris).

Ci-contre en bas : Auguste Renoir, *Le Bal du Moulin de la Galette*, 1876 (musée d'Orsay, Paris).

finissent par se battre en duel. Paul Alexis raconte dans *Le Cri du Peuple* : "Ignorant absolument l'art de l'escrime, Manet et Duranty se jetèrent avec tant de bravoure furieuse l'un sur l'autre que, lorsque les quatre témoins [Zola est un des témoins du peintre] les séparèrent, leurs deux épées se trouvèrent changées en une paire de tire-bouchons. Le soir même, ils étaient devenus les meilleurs amis du monde. Et les habitués du Café Guerbois, heureux et soulagés, composèrent sur eux un triolet de neuf vers." De plus, un nouveau venu, Edgar Degas, n'hésite pas à jeter de l'huile sur le feu. Paul Cézanne, quand il quitte son atelier d'Aix-en-Provence, fait des apparitions pittoresques dans ce chaudron de sorcières de l'art dissident. Dans son roman *L'Œuvre*, Émile Zola évoque ces riches heures. Il rebaptise l'endroit Café Baudequin et n'hésite pas à ironiser sur les participants de ces réunions qui ont changé le cours de l'histoire de l'art en France. La guerre franco-prussienne, puis la Commune dispersent ce qui reste du groupe du Café Guerbois, déjà éclaté en partie lors de la bataille du Salon de 1869 où Manet est une fois de plus refusé. C'est justement cette année-

Chez le Père Lathuile par Édouard Manet, 1879 (musée des Beaux-Arts, Tournai).

là que Manet immortalise l'endroit avec son *Intérieur de café*, un magnifique dessin à l'encre et au crayon.

Le calme revenu, la République proclamée, les anciens du *Guerbois* choisissent un petit établissement tranquille qui ne paye pas de mine de la place Pigalle, au coin de la rue Frochot, le *Café de la Nouvelle-Athènes*. Manet y rassemble ce qui reste de ses amis. Monet,

Sisley se font rares et Pissarro est parti vivre en province. Bazille a été tué au combat pendant le siège de Paris. Cézanne passe de temps à autre. En revanche, Degas, rival déclaré de Manet, a constitué son propre cénacle, entouré de ses jeunes disciples italiens, Diego Marteli, Federico Zandomeneghi et Giuseppe De Nittis. Gustave Caillebotte se plaint de la division

Ci-dessus : Les ruelles de Montmartre ont toujours attiré et inspiré les peintres.

Ci-contre : Dans un café par Gustave Caillebotte, 1880 (musée des Beaux-Arts, Rouen).

Page de droite en haut : Café de Foujita, 1949 (Musée national d'Art Moderne, Paris).

En bas : Dans le jardin du Père Forest, avenue Frochot, Henri de Toulouse-Lautrec fait le portrait de Berthe la Sourde vers 1890.

que ce dernier a provoquée et qui va bientôt être fatale au groupe des impressionnistes : "Degas a apporté la désor-  ganisation parmi nous. C'est très malheureux pour lui qu'il ait le carac- tère si mal fait. Il passe son temps à pérorer à la Nouvelle Athènes ou dans le monde. Il ferait mieux de faire un peu plus de peinture" (lettre à Pissarro). Quoi qu'il en soit, le microcosme de la Nouvelle Athènes est sans aucun doute le salon le plus passionnant de cette époque. Des écri- vains comme Stéphane Mallarmé et Villiers

de L'Isle-Adam, Catulle Mendès et Jean Richepin en sont de fidèles assidus. Le romancier irlandais George Moore, que Manet peint accoudé à un guéridon en 1879, est totalement envoûté par ce lieu qui incarne l'esprit français. C'est encore là que Degas campe l'actrice Ellen Andrée à la terrasse en compagnie de Desboutin dans son célèbre tableau, *Au café*, achevé en 1878. Cependant, Degas s'exile de plus en plus souvent avec ses amis au *Café de La Rochefoucauld*, où le rejoignent Henri de Toulouse-Lautrec,

Alfred Stevens et Guy de Maupassant.

En 1870, un autre café ouvre ses portes place Pigalle, juste en face de la Nouvelle-Athènes. Typique maison dans le style Second Empire, elle porte un nom pour le moins étrange : *Le Rat Mort*. Personne ne sait d'où lui vient cette appellation. On raconte que ce sont les artistes désertant son illustre voisin qui l'ont baptisée ainsi car ils ont jugé qu'on y sentait le rat crevé. Après la Commune, Manet y fait des incursions et Degas y installe sa cour fidèle. L'un et l'autre l'immortalisent dans des compositions, respectivement en 1878 et 1879. Si la *Nouvelle-Athènes* est devenue l'ambassade de l'intelligence et le rendez-vous des poètes symbo-

listes comme des artistes du courant réaliste, *Le Rat Mort* est beaucoup moins bien fréquenté. Verlaine et Rimbaud y viennent en 1872. La chronique se rappelle que c'est à l'une de ses tables que Rimbaud frappe de plusieurs coups de couteau la main de son malheureux compagnon. Jules Vallès, Nadar, Cabaner, Rochefort, Paul Alexis, Daniel Halévy, ami de Degas, François Coppée constituent la clientèle plus ou moins fixe. Le naturalisme y triomphe : Zola et ses disciples donnent le ton jusqu'à la disparition de Manet. Alphonse Allais l'adopte néanmoins quand il n'est pas

à "La Roche", le rendez-vous du Tout-Paris en 1910. Et le café, on ignore pourquoi, devient alors le temple des adeptes de Lesbos, après avoir été l'annexe de *L'Élysée-Montmartre*, qui y a envoyé ses plus sémillantes émissaires.

Les artistes de Montmartre prennent peu à peu la relève dans l'un et l'autre café au début des années quatre-vingt et en changent profondément la physionomie.

C'est à cette période que Montmartre prend son essor. Et celui-ci correspond avec la vogue des tavernes et autres estaminets d'inspiration médiévale, Henri II ou mousquetaire. *Le Cabaret La Grande Pinte*, avenue Trudaine, est l'un des premiers à voir le jour en 1878 sous la direction du père Laplace, ancien marchand de tableaux. Pour décorer la façade, il puise dans l'univers rabelaisien, s'attachant plus particulièrement à l'histoire de Panurge. À l'intérieur, le style est moyen-âgeux et, malgré cela, se révèle somme toute assez confortable. Fréquenté par la bohème, il va être le modèle de la majeure partie des cabarets de la Butte et des abords immédiats.

Toutefois, le véritable inventeur du caractère montmartrois est sans conteste Rodolphe Salis. Peintre qui a jeté ses pinceaux et son chevalet derrière les moulins, fondateur de l'École vibrante et de l'École irisio-subversive, il ouvre un cabaret sur le boulevard Rochechouart et le baptise *Le Chat Noir*, en l'honneur d'Edgar Allan Poe. Il le décore dans le style Louis XIII, recouvrant les murs de tapisseries, de panneaux

CABARET DU NÉANT - Paris-Montmartre — n° 3. Caveau des Trépassés

Ci-dessus : Refuge des poètes et des chansonniers, les cabarets offrent des spectacles variés, des récitals aux saynètes comiques et aux concerts.

Ci-dessous de gauche à droite : La façade de L'Enfer avec ses bas-reliefs de nus féminins en proie aux flammes infernales. Situé à côté, son jumeau, Le Ciel, présentait, à l'inverse des anges. Les garçons, déguisés en squelettes, servaient des boissons imbuvables. La façade du Chat Noir, ancien hôtel particulier du peintre belge Alfred Stevens.

enlevés à de vieux bahuts, un bric-à-brac insensé d'objets. Des meubles massifs, des chaises énormes et des bancs rustiques d'un remarquable inconfort, sont entourés de bibelots en tout genre, de cuirasses, de pots d'étain, de brocs de cuivre et d'armes d'époques diverses. Un gigantesque soleil aux rayons dorés, frappé d'une grosse tête de chat est disposé derrière le comptoir. Les lampes en cuivre sont dessinées par Eugène Grasset. Salis a le sens du théâtre et reçoit ses clients habillé en académicien ou en reître du siècle de Philippe le Bel. Il leur adresse des discours de bienvenue et se met

au piano pour chanter des airs de son cru. Aristide Bruant y fait ses débuts et y connaît un grand succès avec ses chansons de barrières. Il écrit un hymne pour célébrer l'établissement qu'il intitule *Au Chat Noir*. L'ambition de Salis est d'attirer dans son antre les meilleurs éléments de l'élite parisienne et d'en faire une agora nocturne. En réalité, c'est une population hétéroclite qui se presse dans ses salons, du courtier en bourse à l'employé de magasin de nouveautés, des journalistes miteux aux souteneurs. Mais cela n'empêche pas de nombreux clubs d'y trouver refuge, comme l'Acadé-

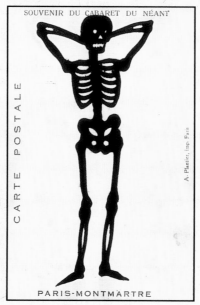

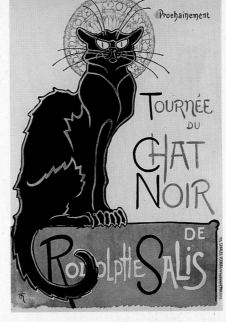

La Tournée du Chat Noir, affiche de Théophile Steinlen, 1896.

Une soirée au Chat Noir en 1900.

mie de la chanson, de la critique, du rire et de l'art sincère. Salis sait aussi séduire les poètes qui viennent lire leurs œuvres au cours de la soirée. Il parvient à débaucher Émile Goudeau et ses Hydropathes, qui officient au Café Vachette, pour qu'ils se produisent chez lui. Il fait aussi venir les Hirsutes, toujours menés par Goudeau, les

Incohérents, placés sous la férule de Jules Lévy, les Harengs Saurs Épileptiques guidés par Paul Signac et Charles Léandre, les Phalanstériens de Montmartre. Sans compter les monologuistes et les chansonniers qu'il recrute pour les vendredis soir qui connaissent un véritable engouement et deviennent rapidement quotidiens.

Un an après la création de son cabaret,

Le Journal du Chat Noir du 29 mars 1886. Cet hebdomadaire tiré à douze mille exemplaires s'offre, entre autres, les contributions régulières d'Alphonse Allais, de Jules Laforgue, de Jules Renard et d'un nombre incalculable d'illustrateurs racontant la vie montmartroise en ce siècle finissant.

Henri de Toulouse-Lautrec est la figure de Montmartre. Aussi bien témoin qu'acteur, il étudiait, dans les cafés et cabarets, le vice et la fête. *Ci-dessus : La Buveuse* ou *La Gueule de bois*, 1889 (musée Toulouse-Lautrec, Albi). Ce dessin représenterait Suzanne Valadon avec qui Lautrec vécut une histoire d'amour passionnée.
Ci-dessous : La Danse au Moulin-Rouge : la Goulue et Valentin le Désossé, 1895 (musée d'Orsay, Paris).

Page de droite : Une autre figure montmartroise : Aristide Bruant et son cabaret.

Salis lance un journal homonyme. Sous une en-tête dessinée par Henri Pille, l'hebdomadaire paraît pendant treize ans. Émile Goudeau, le rédacteur en chef, publie des poèmes et des morceaux en prose de François Coppée, d'Ernest Renan, de Pierre Loti et même de Victor Hugo. Alphonse Allais, champion de l'esprit fumiste, lui succède et y publie les grands illustrateurs de Montmartre, comme Caran d'Ache, Steinlen, Willette, Capy, etc. On y lit alors Paul Verlaine, Jean Moréas, Jules Laforgue et Albert Samain.

Les efforts de Salis sont récompensés : *Le Chat Noir* est désormais le point de ralliement du gotha de la littérature.

Théodore de Banville et Charles Cros, Alphonse Allais, encore étudiant en médecine, et Alphonse Daudet figurent parmi ses illustres habitués.

En 1885, le cabaret déménage et s'installe dans l'ancien atelier du peintre belge Alfred Stevens rue Laval (aujourd'hui rue Victor-Massé). L'architecte Isabey le transforme en hostellerie et la façade, décorée par Henri Pille, est éclairée par deux lanternes d'Eugène Grasset. À l'intérieur, un impressionnant escalier en chêne est construit pour accéder aux étages. La salle du bas, avec une invraisemblable collection d'objets et d'œuvres d'art, est appelée salle Villon et est décorée d'un vitrail dessiné par Willette représentant un veau assis sur un trône installé sur un coffre-fort et s'appuyant contre une guillotine. La salle du conseil se trouve au premier étage, dominée par une cheminée monumentale où se réunit la rédaction du journal, ainsi que l'oratoire. Au second, Georges Rivière installe un théâtre d'ombres.

L'inauguration est marquée par une cérémonie célébrée en grande pompe, avec un suisse, suivi de quatre hallebardiers portant la toile de Willette, *Parce Domine*. Salis, vêtu d'un uniforme de préfet, précède le gérant, en habit de conseiller de préfecture. Et, de nouveau, le succès est au rendez-vous : Tout-Paris accourt pour participer aux festivités du *Chat Noir*.

Des personnalités de tous les milieux et de toutes les conditions composent la foule bigarrée du cabaret : de Ferdinand de Lesseps à Émile Zola, en passant par le célèbre acteur Coquelin et le poète Maurice Donnay. Un subtil mélange de lyrisme et de farce débridée lui donne ce caractère unique. Erik Satie – présenté comme "gymnopédiste" à Salis qui aurait répondu "C'est une bien belle profession" – y joue du piano.

Les représentations du théâtre d'ombres, dont le raffinement et l'invention ne se démentent pas, contribuent à son immense réputation et presque tous les arts sont conviés. Salis a désiré faire de Montmartre le "cerveau du monde". Il n'est pas loin d'avoir atteint son objectif.

L'Auberge du Clou est créée en 1883 par

un brave homme originaire des Grisons. Située en haut de la rue des Martyrs et donnant sur l'avenue Trudaine, elle a de singulier d'instaurer un climat rustique, avec des poutres apparentes, des cheminées paysannes, des nappes à carreaux et des plats de faïence. Les serveurs sont habillés en paysans et des clous servent de patères. Des compositions d'Adolphe Willette décorent la salle. Georges Courteline en fait son second domicile et y installe son célèbre idiomètre pour mesurer la bêtise de ses concitoyens. Satie, qui y travaille comme pianiste après avoir quitté *Le Chat Noir*, y fait la connaissance de Debussy en 1891. Jean Cocteau relate leurs premières rencontres : "Un soir, Erik Satie et Claude Debussy se retrouvent à la même table. Ils sympathisent. Satie demande à Debussy ce qu'il prépare. Debussy compose, comme tout le monde, une wagnerie avec Catulle Mendès. Satie fait la grimace. 'Croyez-moi, murmure-t-il, assez de Wagner ! C'est beau mais pas pour vous'." Un théâtre d'ombres chinoises y est également monté mais seules deux pièces sont présentées, dont une avec la musique de Satie et les décors de Miquel Utrillo.

Ci-dessus : Couverture du journal Le Mirliton par Théophile-Alexandre Steinlen en 1893.

Ci-dessus à droite : Le cabaret des Quat-Zarts et la revue du même nom dont la couverture est dessinée par Adolphe Willette en 1897 (page de droite, en haut).

Ci-contre : Le Rat Mort et l'Abbaye de Thélème. Cette dernière, inspirée par la littérature rabelaisienne, remémore les faits et gestes du bon Panurge.

Quand Rodolphe Salis abandonne l'ancien bureau de poste du boulevard Rochechouart, Aristide Bruant le reprend pour le métamorphoser en un cabaret qu'il appelle Le Mirliton, décoré de nombreux tableaux, dont certains sont de Steinlen et de Toulouse-Lautrec. Ce dernier, fasciné par Bruant l'insolent, y peint des toiles inspirées par ses chansons et déclare lorsqu'il se rend au Mirliton : "Tous les soirs, je vais au bar travailler." Accessible seulement après vingt-deux heures, le visiteur est accueilli par les quolibets et les propos vulgaires du maître de séant. Bruant y sert de la mauvaise bière, insulte le bourgeois et récite des vers hyper-réalistes.

Le 6 octobre 1885, juste en face du Cirque Fernando, la Taverne du Bagne voit le jour boulevard de Clichy. Son propriétaire, Maxime Lisbonne, est un authentique bagnard, condamné à mort en 1871, gracié, puis envoyé au bagne de Toulon, qui a voulu donner à son établissement une atmosphère digne de Cayenne et de toutes les geôles possibles et imaginables. Sa décoration est fruste et pittoresque : une simple baraque en planches, les serveurs vêtus en forçats et les portraits des héros de la Commune épinglés au mur. Lisbonne fait lui aussi imprimer un journal, La Gazette du Bagne, qui a une existence éphémère. Malheureusement, il doit rapidement fermer son étonnante taverne pour tenter ailleurs d'autres expériences.

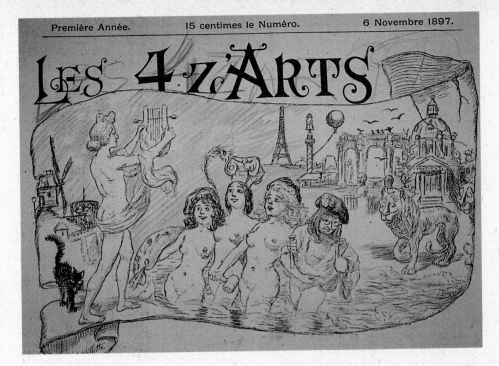

LES 4 z'ARTS

Le Cabaret de l'Abbaye de Thélème vient s'ajouter à ce catalogue baroque de lieux bizarres en 1886. Placé en face du *Café de la Nouvelle-Athènes*, il se distingue par son climat rabelaisien un rien forcé et on le décrit comme étant de style pompéano-moyen-âgeux. Des soirées poétiques y sont organisées et on se presse pour écouter Jean Richepin, Émile Goudeau et Legay. Le vendredi, les dames sont exceptionnellement admises. Des expositions de peintres montmartrois, notamment de Duprelle, y sont organisées de temps à autre.

Le Divan Japonais, sis au n° 75 de la rue des Martyrs, est ouvert en 1888 à l'initiative de Jehan Sarrazin, un poète fantaisiste. C'est d'abord un café musical, où se produit la très célèbre chanteuse Yvette Guilbert, immortalisée par Toulouse-Lautrec, qui dessine son affiche en 1893. Mais les vendredis soir sont réservés à la poésie et à l'art et sont fréquentés par Jean-Louis Forain, Paul Verlaine, Courteline, Alphonse Allais et les chroniqueurs du *Figaro*.

Ce panorama de Montmartre à la Belle Époque ne serait pas complet si l'on oublie de mentionner le *Café Le Tambourin*. Fondé par une belle Italienne du sud, Agostina Segatori, ce petit établissement doit son nom aux instruments de musique accrochés aux murs et aux tables et aux lampes qui ont aussi la forme de tambourins. Son inauguration, le 10 avril 1885, est marquée par une exposition d'œuvres de Gérôme, dont la propriétaire a été le modèle, de Pille, de Clairin, de Février, etc. Elle accueille ses clients en

Ci-dessous : **Affiche du Divan Japonais par Lautrec.**

Ci-dessous : Le Moulin de la Galette et l'affiche dessinée par René Péan en 1898.

Page de droite : Le Moulin-Rouge est en fait un faux moulin – "Ses ailes n'ont jamais moulu que l'argent des clients", disent les méchantes langues... Le jardin comporte un éléphant de carton de l'Exposition Universelle et des divertissements en grand nombre.

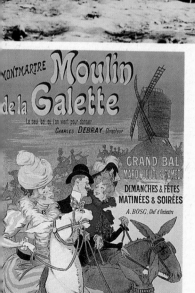

costume folklorique et fait en sorte de recréer un climat méditerranéen. La seconde exposition, présentée en février 1887, est organisée par Vincent Van Gogh, qui habite alors rue Lepic et qui s'est amouraché de la dame napolitaine. Les invités, dont Paul Gauguin, qui exécute deux compositions, *Fleurs et Fruits* et *Fruits*, Émile Bernard, Anquetin, Henri de Toulouse-Lautrec, doivent peindre leurs œuvres sur des toiles rondes en forme de tambourin. Toulouse-Lautrec peint un portrait de Van Gogh assis devant une des tables du café, Vincent exécutant deux portraits de la propriétaire. On trouve parmi ses habitués grand nombre de peintres, dont Steinlen, Forain, Willette, Caran d'Ache, Rollinat, Carabin, mais aussi des écrivains, comme Alphonse Allais. Ambroise Vollard y est passé et rate de peu l'auteur des *Tournesols*. Malheureusement, le petit café d'artistes doit fermer à cause d'une sombre affaire au cours de laquelle Mme Segatori a des ennuis, jamais vraiment clairement élucidés, avec la police.

En 1889, un boucher devenu entrepreneur de spectacles, M. Zidler, fait édifier,

sur l'emplacement de l'ancien Bal de la Reine Blanche, un nouveau lieu de plaisir incandescent qu'il nomme *Moulin-Rouge*. C'est d'abord une très vaste salle de bal mais aussi un agréable jardin, des allées où l'on peut se promener à dos d'âne et assister à des attractions extraordinaires. Sur deux scènes, des artistes se produisent, comme la chanteuse populaire Yvette Guilbert à ses débuts, ou encore La Goulue, chanteuse-étoile du Grand Quadrille et du French cancan, et Valentin le désossé, danseur-acrobate d'une maigreur surréaliste – tout deux immortalisés par Toulouse-Lautrec. Bientôt le Tout-Paris se précipite pour se divertir dans cette atmosphère hyper-naturaliste où s'exhibent des ballerines délurées comme Rayon-d'Or, la Môme Fromage et Grille d'Égout, Vestris et autres vestales de ce temple des dépravations.

Toulouse-Lautrec, comme Auguste Renoir, a également une prédilection pour *Le Moulin de la Galette* où le petit peuple des Batignolles et du Faubourg Saint-Antoine vient danser la polka, la valse et le quadrille dans une atmosphère bon enfant.

Aristide Bruant, qui incarne désormais la veine gouailleuse et tragique de ce Montmartre frondeur, refuge de l'anticonformisme dans une ère on ne peut plus conformiste, décide de racheter en 1903 le vieux *Cabaret des Assassins*, un charmant séjour encore campagnard sis rue des Saules, tout en haut de la Butte, administré par Adèle, une ancienne danseuse de cancan. André Gill se voit confier la responsabilité de peindre l'enseigne du nouvel établissement. Il a l'idée de montrer un lapin habillé en apache qui danse dans une casserole en brandissant une bouteille de vin devant un moulin. "Le lapin à Gill" se transforme très vite en "Lapin Agile", d'où le nom de l'établissement. Le séjour est assez plaisant pour attirer les héros de la bohème fin de siècle et des personnages amoureux des arts modernes : Georges Courteline, Alphonse Allais, Caran d'Ache, Auguste Renoir, Georges Clemenceau. Bruant confie la maison à une figure haute en couleur, un peu peintre, un peu céramiste, vaguement poète, qui vit entouré de son chien, de son corbeau et de son âne, un certain Frédéric Gérard. Celui que tout le monde surnomme Frédé, chante le soir pour divertir ses clients, choisissant à dessein un répertoire désuet, et a l'idée d'organiser des lectures de poésie des plus informelles où de jeunes inconnus peuvent se produire. Des comédiens débutants y prennent part, comme Charles Dullin, mais les vrais poètes, qui viennent nombreux, se gardent bien de monter sur l'estrade pour déclamer. Roland Dorgelès, Guillaume Apollinaire, Francis Carco, André Salmon, Max Jacob, Pierre Mac Orlan prennent un malin plaisir à assister à ces exhibitions souvent pathétiques ou comiques.

C'est au *Lapin Agile* que Dorgelès a l'idée de monter le plus remarquable canular de l'époque des grandes révolutions esthétiques : ne cessant de se chamailler avec son collègue Apollinaire (ils écrivent tous deux dans les colonnes de *Paris Journal*) à propos de l'art moderne, il lui passe par la tête de faire produire un tableau par l'âne Aliboron, dit Lolo, le compagnon de Frédé, qu'il rebaptise pour l'occasion de l'anagramme

La Goulue (photographiée ci-dessus) et vue par Lautrec sur une affiche pour le Moulin-Rouge en 1891 (en bas).

Page de droite :
Yvette Guilbert. Cette chanteuse, qui a été une des étoiles du Montmartre de Lautrec, incarne la gouaille cynique et un peu morbide qui fait les délices des habitants des quartiers sages de la capitale.

vibrant de l'école "excessiviste", est présenté au Salon des Indépendants, où il est acheté par un collectionneur pour la somme non indifférente de 500 F. Il faut se souvenir qu'à ce moment-là, les artistes les plus audacieux, ceux qui inventent le cubisme, vivent de façon assez misérable dans le Bateau-Lavoir de la rue Ravignan, et que Montmartre s'est imposé comme la forteresse des idées transgressives en peinture et en sculpture. Amedeo Modigliani, Suzanne Valadon et son fils Maurice Utrillo, Picasso, Juan Gris, André Derain, Kees Van Dongen, sont des habitués du petit cabaret décoré de dessins et de toiles d'un certain nombre d'entre eux. C'est en ces lieux que le collectionneur allemand, Wilhelm Uhde, retrouve la trace de l'auteur inconnu du tableau le *Tub* acheté dans une galerie et qui n'est autre que Picasso. La réussite de la plupart de ces créateurs transforme le *Lapin Agile* en sanctuaire accueillant des pèlerins venus des quatre coins du globe.

D'autres cafés de Montmartre ont tenu une place conséquente dans l'aventure du cubisme. C'est le cas de *L'Ami Émile*, de l'autre côté de la place Ravignan. Marcoussis et Juan Gris décorent de panneaux mirobolants cette académie artistique. Picasso, en compagnie de son ami Max Jacob, retrouve ses camarades espagnols, Sabartès, Soto, Manolo, au *Zut*, place Jean-Baptiste-Clément, dont la clientèle est pour l'essentiel constituée d'anarchistes, qui a

Boronali. Il rédige alors une parodie de manifeste clamant : "Holà ! grands peintres excessifs, mes frères. Holà ! pinceaux rénovateurs. Brisons la palette archaïque et posons les principes de la peinture de demain. Notre formule sera l'excessivisme. L'excès en art est une force. Le soleil n'est jamais trop ardent, le ciel trop vert, la mer trop rouge. [...]" Son tableau, baptisé très pompeusement *Soleil sur l'Adriatique*, manifeste

été gouverné par Frédé avant sa promotion au *Lapin Agile*. *Le Téléphone*, un bistrot sans qualité en haut de la rue Lepic, reçoit aussi bien Paul Fort que les habitants du Bateau-Lavoir.

Mais le café qui réunit toute la galaxie artistique de Montmartre autour de 1910 est sans conteste le *Café de l'Ermitage* du boulevard de Rochechouart. Sur sa terrasse on peut y voir, Marinetti assis à côté de Georges Braque, Marie Laurencin auprès d'Ardengo Soffici, Pablo Gargallo conversant avec Picasso, Fernand Léger en face de Gino Severini, Francis Picabia non loin d'Umberto Boccioni. Fernande Olivier, compagne de Picasso raconte : "On s'y coudoyait sans se parler et chaque groupe avait sa place attitrée. On y vit quelques batailles et c'est même la seule fois que nous vîmes, Braque et moi, Picasso se fâcher contre un consommateur qui l'avait poussé un peu brutalement et lui décocha un direct dans la mâchoire. Braque se hâta se séparer les combattants au grand dommage de l'adversaire de Picasso." Sans compter tous les nouveaux émules du cubisme, évoluant au milieu de mauvais garçons sortis des romans de Carco et de Mac Orlan, qui s'éloignent pour se réfugier dans l'un des derniers endroits authentiques de la Commune libre, *La Maison Rouge*.

Au milieu des années vingt, les surréalistes, qui n'aiment pas arpenter les sentiers

L'enseigne du Lapin Agile a donné son nom à l'établissement. Elle résume la légende de Montmartre et l'esprit du lieu volontairement campagnard et anticonformiste.

Ci-contre : Le Lapin Agile vu par Élisée Maclet en 1920 (collection particulière, Paris).

battus, élisent un bien banal café du boulevard, situé à côté du Moulin-Rouge, *Le Cyrano*. En rangs serrés à la terrasse, ils rédigent des lettres d'insulte aux écrivains et aux peintres à succès, aux critiques de tous bords, ou ils s'entassent dans l'arrière-salle, véritable poudrière, pour tenir leurs assises. Marcel Duhamel relate quelques épisodes tumultueux dans *Raconte pas ta vie* : "Un brusque tohu-bohu de voix excitées, de chaises renversées et de verres cassés s'élève au sein du groupe. Un prêtre en soutane vient d'avoir l'idée saugrenue de s'asseoir parmi nous. Mû par le fameux réflexe anticureton, Benjamin Péret s'est levé et l'a giflé. Breton, furieux, intervient, sépare les combattants…" ou encore "Un autre jour, c'est toujours Péret qui proteste, mais là il n'est pas le seul, quand Breton se lève pour serrer la main à un monsieur assez corpulent en pardessus sombre et feutre bleu, arborant la rosette à la boutonnière. C'est Léon-Paul Fargue, que Breton se refuse à cataloguer parmi les nuisibles." C'est là que seront excommuniés Antonin Artaud et Philippe Soupault en 1926. Philippe Soupault s'est lassé de l'organisation du Cyrano : "Je n'étais pas le seul à vouloir refuser cette discipline, ces obligations, ces rencontres avec les mêmes participants. Tous

La cour du Lapin Agile.
Aliboron, l'âne du
propriétaire, devint célèbre
sous le nom de Joachim-
Raphaël Boronali pour
avoir peint, avec sa queue
et avec l'aide de Dorgelès,
auteur de la supercherie,
un tableau. Cette œuvre
fut exposée au Salon des
Indépendants et vendue
à un collectionneur pour
la somme de cinq cents
francs. "Un âne chef
d'école."

Ci-contre :
Une soirée au Lapin Agile
avant 1914.

les soirs et même tous les matins au café de la place Blanche. Des jugements. "Et que devient X ou Y ? Il y a longtemps qu'on ne l'a pas vu celui-là." Insupportable. Injustifiable." Au petit bistrot de la place Blanche, à deux pas de la maison d'André Breton rue Fontaine, le rituel des apéritifs se répète invariablement. Autour de Breton, qui trône en monarque absolu, ses disciples et amis sirotent des Mandarin-Curaçao et des Claquesin ou des Picon. Marcel Duhamel, Benjamin Péret, parfois Giorgio De Chirico, Maxime Alexandre, Jacques Prévert, Max Ernst, Raymond Queneau, Yves Tanguy, pour ne citer qu'eux, ont pris part ou ont été témoins de ces scéances quotidiennes où le surréalisme ne s'est pas encore mis corps et âme au service de la révolution.

L'étoile de Montmartre pâlit à mesure que ses peintres entrent dans l'histoire du XXᵉ siècle. Toutefois, son mythe est si puissant qu'il a réussi à subsister jusqu'à nos jours.

De tous les artistes qui ont choisi Montmartre comme patrie, Maurice Utrillo a certainement été celui qui a exalté ce quartier avec le plus de ferveur.

Ci-dessus : Maurice Utrillo par Suzanne Valadon en 1910.

Ci-contre : Une rue de Montmartre par Maurice Utrillo (collection particulière).

Page de droite : Maurice Utrillo et Suzanne Valadon (tournant la tête) dans un café de Montmartre.

MONTMARTRE DE

J'ai toujours trouvé
que la plus belle vue sur
Paris était à Montmartre.
Mais la raison pour
laquelle j'ai choisi d'y
habiter tient justement aux
bistrots. Ce quartier
a été dès le départ
construit autour des
bistrots. Dans ce quartier
tout le monde se prend
pour un artiste. Les voisins
ne sont pas des voisins,

Claude Lelouch

Ce sont des artistes
qui ont des conversations
d'artistes.
À Montmartre,
on a une vie d'artiste — et
les artistes vont au bistrot.
C'est dans les bistrots
que j'ai souvent pioché
la plupart de mes dialogues
et sûrement les plus belles
répliques de mes films.

Mars 1998

Moi, j'ai toujours espéré étant à Paris avoir une exposition
dans un café…

Vincent Van Gogh

On voyait qu'il y avait là une ambiance très différente de celle des grands boulevards, mais je ne pouvais pas me rendre compte encore de quelle vie intense et intéressante elle était faite. Dans ces petites rues qui presque toutes menaient à la grande église du Sacré-Cœur alors en construction (…) on savait, et cela se savait aussi en Italie, que dans toute cette personnalité bouillait un esprit révolutionnaire contre l'académie qui imprégnait tout Montmartre.

Gino Severini

Rien ne ressemblait moins à un quartier de Paris que
cette paroisse attardée, [...] Passé la rue Lepic, on
renonçait aux usages courants. Chacun agissait à sa
guise, se fichant du tiers comme du quart.

Jean Renoir

L'hiver est des plus doux et, à la terrasse de ce café voué au commerce des stupéfiants, les femmes font des apparitions courtes et charmantes [...] Je ne me souviens pas d'avoir vécu ailleurs.

André Breton

37

[Le surréalisme] ne s'écrit pas, ne se peint pas. Il se vit, et ils sont autant d'apôtres d'une nouvelle religion qui se célèbre dans les cafés.

Maurice Nadeau

Ce petit paradis de lilas
et de rose semblait le bout
du monde…

Jean Renoir

39

À l'angle de la rue Saint-Vincent,
endormie derrière ses palissades, la
terrasse vous attend sous le maigre
feuillage d'un acacia torturé. Incrusté
pour ainsi dire sur le côté boisé de la
Butte, ce cabaret est si tranquille que
Salz, son premier propriétaire, sous-chef
de bureau à la mairie de Montmartre,
l'avait d'abord baptisé À ma campagne.

Francis Carco

Au Bateau-Lavoir, oui j'étais célèbre ! Quand Uhde venait du fond de l'Allemagne pour voir mes peintures, quand les peintres de tous les pays m'apportaient ce qu'ils faisaient, me demandaient des conseils, quand je n'avais pas le sou, là, j'étais célèbre. J'étais un peintre, pas une bête curieuse.

Pablo Picasso

MONTPARNASSE.

AU CAFFE' DU PARNASSE

GERARD PHILIPE
LILLI PALMER

Montparnasse 19

HIER ...

La commune de Montrouge, qui voit le jour au début de la Révolution, ne doit sa réputation qu'à de bien tristes circonstances. Elle est en effet connue pour abriter des hôpitaux qui soignent les maladies vénériennes, à commencer par l'hôpital du Midi ou des hospices où l'on enferme les fous, tel l'établissement de Sainte-Anne. Et c'est place Saint-Jacques que se dresse la guillotine, attirant des foules de badauds qui veulent assister à l'exécution de Lacenaire ou des criminels entre 1832 et 1852.

Toute la partie de Montrouge qui se trouve à l'intérieur des fortifications de Thiers est rattachée à Paris en 1860 pour constituer le XIVe arrondissement, alors appelé le quartier de l'Observatoire. Les grands travaux d'urbanisme conduits par le baron Haussmann qui métamorphosent les dix arrondissements originels de la capitale font refluer dans cette zone un nombre important d'artisans et de petites industries. La mécanique et l'imprimerie, puis la production des appareillages électriques s'y développent. Ébénistes et menuisiers, maréchaux-ferrants et voituriers s'installent aussi dans les ateliers de Plaisance ou du Petit Montrouge. Des brasseries apparaissent même vers les années quatre-vingt-dix.

Rien dans tout cela n'explique le brusque engouement suscité par Montparnasse, qui attire à l'aube de notre siècle une cohorte d'artistes qui font dissidence et abandonnent les rues pentues, les cabarets et la misère de Montmartre. Il est vrai que des peintres et des sculpteurs se sont déjà incrustés dans ces faubourgs industrieux au cours du siècle précédent : le passage des Arts à Plaisance et la rue des Artistes à Montsouris en témoignent amplement. Le sculpteur Bartholdi y prépare la statue de la Liberté et le Douanier Rousseau y passe une partie de

Pages précédentes :
La barrière du Maine.

Page de gauche : **Le café du Parnasse, anciennement café Vavin, est le premier à Montparnasse à exposer des tableaux sur ses murs. La première exposition se tient en 1921. Cette pratique sera rapidement adoptée par les établissements alentour.**

Ci-dessus : **Affiche du film** *Montparnasse 19* **de Jacques Becker qui retrace la vie de Modigliani d'après l'ouvrage du critique d'art Michel Georges-Michel** *Les Montparnos.*

sa triste existence. Le théâtre conquiert aussi la rue de la Gaîté, comme la Gaîté-Montparnasse et le théâtre Montparnasse, où Antoine monte son Théâtre Libre pendant la saison 1887-1888. Mais peut-être est-ce Aristide Bruant qui chante ses refrains sinistres et gouailleurs au *Mirliton*, et triomphe avec *À Montrouge !* et *À Montmartre !*, qui réussit à rendre populaires ces rues où roôdent les apaches.

Quoi qu'il en soit, la bohème y a pris pied au milieu des immigrés arrivés des ghettos des pays baltes ou des régions pauvres de l'Espagne et les tristes troquets de la place Vavin, qui n'a, jusqu'au percement du boulevard Raspail en 1911, vraiment rien de remarquable.

À cette époque, la nouvelle bohème croît dans la plus joyeuse dissipation autour de la Sorbonne et surtout le long du

Boul'Mich', hantant le *Caveau du Soleil d'Or*, le *Café Vachette* ou le *Café d'Harcourt*. Écrivains et peintres colonisent aussi les terrasses du Luxembourg. Mais un endroit a la faveur d'un grand nombre de poètes, qui n'hésitent pas à abandonner leurs points de ralliement favoris pour se réunir à l'ombre de la statue du maréchal Ney, tirant son sabre au clair pour l'éternité. Cet endroit s'appelle *La Closerie des Lilas*.

Située en face du *Bal Bullier*, *La Closerie* est, à l'origine, une petite guinguette tout ce qu'il y a de plus champêtre, plantée dans un paysage de cerisiers et de vergers qui enchante Honoré de Balzac. François-René de Chateaubriand apprécie cet endroit quand il veut échapper à sa retraite de la rue d'Enfer. C'est le premier relais de poste sur la route de Fontainebleau qui se dresse dans un jardin idyllique où le lilas fleurit sur des tonnelles en lourdes grappes à la fragrance têtue. Léon Daudet aime y flâner au milieu de modestes employés, d'étudiants et de révolutionnaires russes. Les poètes Raoul Ponchon et Jean Richepin fréquentent ce havre de paix loin des rumeurs de la ville.

Un homme, un seul, en change de façon profonde et irréversible la physionomie : le poète Paul Fort. En 1901, entraîné par l'écrivain symboliste américain Stuart Merrill, il adopte le *Café de Versailles*, en face de la gare Montparnasse, dont la façade fut transpercée par une locomotive endiablée. Il y rencontre des artistes norvégiens et les étudiants scandinaves de l'éphémère Académie créée par Matisse qui vont y prendre racine. Mais Paul Fort l'abandonne en 1903 pour débarquer avec armes et bagages à *La Closerie des Lilas*, dont plus rien ni personne ne le fera

Ci-contre : 25 octobre 1895, un train transperce la façade du Café de Versailles place de Rennes (aujourd'hui place du 18-juin-1940 en face de la gare Montparnasse. Ce café fut l'annexe de l'Académie Matisse située non loin.

Page de droite : *Le Bal Bullier* par Ludovic Valée, 1902 (musée Carnavalet, Paris).
La façade du Bullier, le plus ancien bal de Paris, avenue de l'Observatoire.

partir. Et quand il prend la direction de la revue littéraire *Vers et Prose* deux ans plus tard, il reçoit ses amis et les auteurs désireux de le rencontrer tous les mardis à heure fixe. Vêtu de son éternelle redingote boutonnée jusqu'au col orné de son éternelle cravate noire, il attire à lui des hordes d'écrivains venus de tous les horizons, des Russes, des Suédois, des Espagnols, des Polonais, le nec plus ultra de la poésie française, Jean Moréas en tête, Jules Laforgue, Gustave Kahn, Maurice Raynal, Napoléon Roinard. Roland Dorgelès, André Billy, André Salmon et Francis Carco encore à leurs débuts, sont familiers de ces rencontres. Rubén Dario et O.V. Milocz, Saint-Pol Roux et Jules Romains

Prince des poètes, Paul Fort
s'affirme l'âme de la
Closerie des Lilas (ici à la
terrasse en 1920). Il y reçoit
les écrivains et les artistes
du monde entier. Les
représentants du Parnasse,
du naturalisme, du
symbolisme, du cubisme,
du futurisme et de tous
les autres «ismes» du
début du XXᵉ siècle n'ont
pas manqué de se
retrouver à l'occasion
des mardis de cette figure
attachante et généreuse
de la poésie française.

La terrasse très animée de la Closerie des Lilas en 1925. À ce moment-là, ce grand café, déjà chargé d'un lourd passé, est fréquenté par les surréalistes qui n'hésitent pas à y faire scandale.

les rejoignent. Max Jacob ne manque jamais une occasion de s'y faire remarquer par ses excentricités. Les revues s'y font représenter ponctuellement : Guillaume Apollinaire y entraîne l'équipe des *Soirées de Paris*, la rédaction de la *Revue Blanche*, conduite par Vielé-Griffin répond toujours présent ainsi que les collaborateurs du *Mercure de France*, derrière Charles Morice et Van Bever. Même les figures emblématiques du Boulevard, intriguées par la rumeur provenant de ce point reculé de la rive gauche, quittent le *Café Napolitain* pour observer la faune extraordinaire qui a envahi ce qui ressemble de plus en plus au quartier général de la jeune littérature.

Paul Fort est élu prince des poètes en 1912 et il exerce désormais sa magistrature intellectuelle incontestée.

La Closerie des Lilas est le centre névralgique de la création dans le monde et personne ne veut rater ce rendez-vous avec l'histoire. Même ceux qui ne se sentent pas d'affinités électives avec les légions poétiques de Paul Fort ne veulent pas être de reste : Paul Léautaud se place en embuscade derrière une table au fond de la salle et note dans son Journal : "Je me suis laissé aller ce soir à la réunion de *Vers et Prose* à *La Closerie des Lilas* ayant reçu une invitation de Paul Fort. C'est bien la première et dernière fois. [...] Paul Fort était aussi un peu ivre, parlait tout de travers. Tout ce monde ne quitte guère le café. Le plus surprenant c'est qu'ils n'ont pas l'air de s'embêter." André Gide s'y rend en 1906 en la compagnie austère de Jean Schlumberger et des Van Rysselberghe.

Beaucoup de peintres et de sculpteurs, comme Charles Guérin, le Norvégien Diriks, le Suédois Carle Palme et d'autres, ne tardent pas à rejoindre ce cercle brillant et turbulent, qui finit par former une véritable armée. Dans ses rangs on commence à discerner les maîtres de la nouvelle donne esthétique, comme Pablo Picasso, introduit dans ce vaste caravansérail de l'esprit par le bon Guillaume Apollinaire. L'avant-garde artistique est également de la partie. Les trois frères Villon, Marcel Duchamp, Jacques Villon et Duchamp-Villon, Fernand Léger, Constantin Brancusi, Albert Gleizes, Metzinger, Le Fauconnier assistent également aux célèbres mardis. Bon nombre d'Italiens considèrent qu'ils doivent faire leur classe dans cette "boîte enchantée d'où s'élancerait, selon André Salmon, le génie de la Renaissance montparnasienne". L'artiste et homme de lettres Ardengo Soffici retrouve là

Fernand Léger en 1952.
Dans un café et dans son atelier du 86 de la rue Notre-Dame-des-Champs.

Ci-dessus : André Breton
lors d'un meeting en 1948.

Ci-contre : Louis Aragon
en 1945.

Page de droite en haut :
Max Ernst et Paul Éluard.

En bas : Pablo Picasso,
Louis Aragon, Elsa Triolet,
Jean Cocteau et Maurice
Thorez en 1956.

ses compatriotes et le philosophe toscan Giovanni Papini. Les peintres Carlo Carrà et Gino Severini, qui épousera Jeanne, la fille du maître de céans, sans oublier Filippo Tommaso Marinetti viennent y jeter la bombe du futurisme. Après la Grande Guerre, les résidents de *La Closerie des Lilas* changent en partie. Des Anglo-Saxons y cherchent leurs marques, comme Ernest Hemingway qui s'entretient là avec Ford Madox Ford, l'auteur du *Bon soldat*, ou avec

Ezra Pound. MM. les Dadas tentent de s'insinuer dans ce gigantesque panorama culturel et Louis Aragon est le premier à en franchir le seuil en 1919. Ils ne tardent pas à le changer en ring idéologique. Arrivé depuis peu en France, le poète roumain fondateur du mouvement dada, Tristan Tzara empêche André Breton, avec lequel il vient de rompre de manière spectaculaire, d'organiser un important rassemblement international convoquant tous les mouvements d'avant-garde. Il bat le rappel de ses troupes à la *Closerie* et rédige une déclaration qui retire sa confiance aux organisations du Congrès de Paris. Cette scission marque la fin du dadaïsme en France. Breton écrit le *Premier Manifeste du surréalisme* en 1924 et lance ainsi un mouvement qui va conquérir plusieurs continents. En sorte que

Paris reste aux commandes de la nef de la modernité : *Fluctuat nec mergitur !*

La *Closerie des Lilas* ne peut échapper au besoin absolu qu'ont les surréalistes de faire scandale et d'épater le bourgeois. Le banquet organisé au début du mois de juillet 1925 en l'honneur de Saint-Pol Roux est l'occasion rêvée pour semer la zizanie. Rachilde, l'épouse de Valette, le directeur du *Mercure de France*, auteur à succès, a tenu des propos chauvins qui exaspèrent les amis de Breton. Les surréalistes décident donc de perturber cette cérémonie, insultant la dame de lettres et provoquant finalement une bagarre générale. Max Ernst hurle : "À bas l'Allemagne !" et Michel Leiris, évitant de justesse de se faire lyncher, vocifère : "À bas la France !". Philippe Soupault raconte : "Breton se précipita par la fenêtre et, je ne sais comment, réussit à détacher les volets, et, de mon côté, à la poursuite d'un journaliste, je me suis pendu au lustre et me balançai, ce qui me permit de balayer toute la vaisselle et les verres du banquet. Sur ces entrefaites, un car de police arriva. Les agents de police cernèrent la Closerie des Lilas." Louis Aragon raconte que c'est dans ce tumulte échevelé qu'il rencontre pour la première fois Elsa Triolet, envoyée là par son pays pour le séduire. Plusieurs surréalistes sont blessés ou finissent au poste.

L'histoire de cet établissement célèbre ne s'arrête pas à cette date. Mais jamais plus il ne connaîtra une telle amplitude dans la géopolitique de la culture parisienne. Pendant les années soixante-dix et au début des années quatre-vingt, on peut y voir, le soir, Philippe Sollers et les collaborateurs de *Tel*

À la Rotonde tous les artistes qui se reconnaissent dans l'avènement de l'art moderne marquent leur territoire.

Ci-dessous : De gauche à droite, Ortiz de Zarate, Max Jacob, Moïse Kisling, Pâquerette (modèle chez Poiret), Marie Vassilieff et Picasso réunis en 1916.

Quel, Jean-Edern Hallier, Jacques Lacan et le clan des psychanalystes de son école et des auditeurs de son séminaire. Sotto voce, *La Closerie* poursuit sa carrière exceptionnelle.

Pendant que *La Closerie des Lilas* catalyse les énergies poétiques avant que n'éclate le grand conflit européen, Montparnasse change peu à peu de physionomie. On afflue de partout pour communier dans cette internationale du cube et de la couleur pure. *Le Petit Napolitain* accueille les amis de la revue *Vers et Prose*, les membres de l'Académie de l'Humour et le petit groupe belge de la *Feuille littéraire*. Quelques vieux poètes, transfuges du Quartier latin aiment à s'y fréquenter, comme le "poète-agent" Viélé-Griffin, policier de son état, ou Ernest Raynaud. Bientôt les premiers cubistes se rencontrent au *Café du Parnasse*, ancien *Café Vavin*, le premier établissement à organiser une exposition de groupe en 1921, avec d'ailleurs un certain retentissement puisqu'on y voit des œuvres de Gontcharova, de Soutine, de Nina Hamnett, d'Ortiz de Zarate.

La Rotonde n'est encore qu'un bistroquet d'ouvriers ou de cochers de fiacre, avec son comptoir en zinc. En 1911, un certain Victor Libion le rachète et l'agrandit. Sympathique citoyen de l'Auvergne, Libion parvient à attirer chez lui ces expatriés, leur offrant l'illusion d'y trouver une chaleur familiale et un authentique respect. En sorte qu'une multitude de Latino-Américains, de Scandinaves, d'Espagnols, de Russes com-

Amedeo Modigliani en 1910
à la terrasse de la Rotonde
avec Adolphe Basler,
à droite.
L'artiste livournais a élu
la Rotonde comme son
second domicile. Il y est
protégé par le patron qui
le traite comme son fils
adoptif.
Ci-dessous :
Dans son atelier.

mencent à affluer dans la modeste maison de celui qu'ils surnomment "Papa Libion". Au bout de quelques mois on "apollinarise" et le futurisme y est de règle, comme d'ailleurs tous les autres *ismes* de l'époque. Maurice de Vlaminck peut alors s'écrier à juste titre : "Montparnasse, c'était la Rotonde" ! La nouvelle a d'ores et déjà fait le tour du globe.

Le *Café de la Rotonde*, qu'on appelle ironiquement le "Raspail-Plage", est devenu, en moins de temps qu'il ne faut pour le dire, une foire monumentale avec les personnages les plus pittoresques qu'on puisse imaginer se mêlant aux personnalités du Salon d'Automne ou du Salon des Indépendants. Personne ne veut rater le spectacle et encore moins ne pas y figurer. Arthur Cravan, qui annonce l'imminence de son prochain match de boxe, côtoie le très surprenant Chilien Manuel Ortiz de Zarate, assistant, durant l'été 1916, de Picasso et qui se dit le "seul Patagon de Paris", Jean Giraudoux y scrute les nouvelles mœurs parisiennes et Apollinaire prêche l'évangile des temps nouveaux. Une catégorie inconnue d'individus est apparue : les "Rotondistes". Parmi eux, on distingue des

êtres fantasques et désespérés, comme le bel Amedeo Modigliani, déclamant des strophes de la *Divine Comédie*, que Libion protège du mieux qu'il peut, incapable cependant de le sauver de ses vices. La faune évoluant à la terrasse ou dans la salle enfumée forme le parlement qui édicte les lois de l'iconoclastie moderniste. On y retrouve Pablo Picasso, André Derain, Juan Gris, Lipchitz, André Lhote, Kisling, mais aussi Ramòn Gòmez de la Serna, Francis Carco, Léon-Paul Fargue, André Salmon, Ilya Ehrenbourg, le musicien Georges Auric, au milieu de modèles plus ou moins dévergondées échappées de la Grande Chaumière – la petite académie de peinture qui

Les artistes et
intellectuels de toutes
les nationalités
se regroupent
aux terrasses de
Montparnasse.
Ils forment des cercles
en fonction de leurs
origines et de leurs
langues. Les Polonais
(*ci-contre*) privilégient
la Rotonde, les
Allemands s'installent
au Dôme et les écrivains
américains apprécient
plutôt le Sélect.

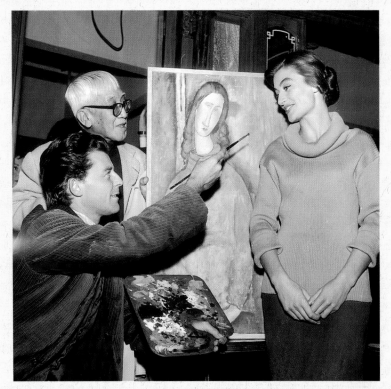

Ci-dessus : **Gérard Philipe, Anouk Aimée et Foujita lors du tournage du film *Montparnasse 19* en 1957.**

Ci-dessous : **Carrefour international le Dôme peut être considéré comme un véritable microcosme.**

fournit le premier contingent de Montparnos – et de journalistes en quête de sensationnel. Et les révolutions, réelles ou imaginaires, se préparent dans un coin du café où Lénine conspire avec Léon Trotski.

La guerre entraîne la majorité des "Rotondistes" dans les tranchées. La plupart des étrangers se portent volontaires. Même Modigliani se présente devant les autorités militaires, qui le renvoient dans ses foyers. Seul Picasso, qui déteste la France, rôde encore chez Libion où règne une atmosphère étrange d'espionnite. Le 1er août 1916, Jean Cocteau réalise un reportage photographique où les permissionnaires et ceux qui sont restés à l'arrière, se retrouvent pour oublier le drame mondial. Salmon, Kisling, Picasso, Modigliani, Ortiz de Zarate, Marie Vassilieff, Henri-Pierre Roché en uniforme, Pâquerette, le mannequin vedette de Paul Poiret, se mettent en scène à la terrasse du café ou dans un rayon d'action qui n'excède

pas les limites du carrefour Vavin. Ces documents extraordinaires prouvent que le cercle magique n'a pas été rompu par la terrible réalité du conflit qui est en train de modifier la carte du monde et d'en rayer les plus puissants empires.

L'École de Paris tient bon et la bohème cosmopolite demeure fidèle à La Rotonde. Le succès prodigieux de l'endroit ne se dément pas, mais va bientôt lui être fatal. Francis Picabia et Igor Stravinsky l'adoptent à leur tour, tout comme le vieux sculpteur Bourdelle, le mondain Kees Van Dongen, le jeune artiste tchèque Joseph Sima et Maurice Utrillo, toujours entre deux vins, quand il abandonne son atelier montmartrois. Le café est un des objectifs des touristes après la tour Eiffel et le musée du Louvre. Michel-Georges Michel, en publiant en 1923 *Les Montparnos*, le classe une fois pour toute dans la mythologie du XXe siècle. Et c'est bien là

le drame : les plus fidèles habitués doivent céder le terrain à ces vagues ininterrompues d'intrus et de curieux qui déferlent à sa terrasse, sans compter le dancing qui donne le coup de grâce. Les beaux jours sont révolus : les "Rotondistes" ont traversé le boulevard.

L'histoire du *Café du Dôme* est intimement liée à l'arrivée inopinée des rapins dans cette partie encore peu considérée de la rive gauche même s'il existe déjà avant *La Rotonde*. M. Chambon, le nouveau patron auvergnat, voit tout le profit qu'il peut tirer du succès de son voisin. Il s'y fonde une agora, d'abord monopolisée par les élèves, venus du nord et de l'est de l'Europe, de Matisse qui, pressé de créer une académie, enseigne à partir de 1908 dans un atelier du boulevard des Invalides. Les Allemands, surtout des collaborateurs de la revue satirique *Simplicissimus*, et tous ceux qui ne se reconnaissent pas dans la lame de fond expressionniste élisent la terrasse du *Dôme* comme forum. La bohème des artistes, qui compte le Bulgare Pascin et le Tchèque Georges Kars, puis des Anglais, des Améri-

Ci-contre : Jean-Louis Forain, *L'Absinthe*, 1885 (musée Marmottan, Paris).

Ci-dessous : Le Dôme.

Le Dôme.
Ci-dessus : 1910. Jules Pascin, Rudolf Levy, Walter Bondy et Wilhelm Uhde.

Ci-dessous : 1900. De gauche à droite, Madame Bondy et Walter Bondy, Jules Pascin, Hermine David et Walter Rosam.

Page de droite : La terrasse en 1959.

cains, des Italiens, est suivie des hordes de parasites et d'excentriques complétant la composition bigarrée de cette terrasse alternative à celle de *La Rotonde*. Une expression voit le jour : on parle des "Dômiers" comme on parle des "Rotondistes". Pendant les années vingt, la terrasse ne désemplit jamais. Maïakovski s'installe à la table voisine de celle de Sylvia Beach, dont la librairie de la rue de l'Odéon *Shakespeare & Company* devient très rapidement un lieu de rencontres exceptionnelles, ou de celle du couple Desnos-Youki. En 1928, les frères Pierre et Jacques Prévert y tournent une séquence de leur film, *Paris la belle*. Mais déjà le Dôme n'est

plus que l'ombre de lui-même et une foule de faux artistes et de faux poètes a remplacé les premiers venus qui ont fait sa gloire.

De l'illustre trio du carrefour, *Le Sélect* est le petit cadet. Ouvert en 1924, il recueille les fruits de ces années héroïques qui ont élevé Montparnasse à la dignité de capitale incontestée de l'art. Les émigrés provenant de toutes les nations d'Europe et des Amériques s'y sentent à l'aise. Cet asile polyglotte, unique en son genre, accueille toute la "génération perdue", expression créée, d'après Hemingway, par le garagiste de Gertrude Stein. Pour rencontrer les romanciers, les poètes, les essayistes de

l'étranger, nul besoin de voyager, il suffit de pousser la porte de ce café et de s'asseoir à l'une des tables ou sur l'un des tabourets du bar. Faculté est alors offerte de côtoyer Hart Crane, l'auteur du *Pont*, l'extravagant Francis Scott Fitzgerald, Malcolm Cowley, Louis Bromfield, Richard McAlmon, l'un des plus solides piliers, E. E. Cummings qui rêve à ses poèmes typographiés, ou encore Gershwin qui chante les thèmes d'*Un Américain à Paris*. Au *Sélect*, William Carlos Williams s'entretient avec Philippe Soupault, et William Faulkner, à l'époque où il vit rue Servandoni, ne dédaigne pas d'y consommer quelques verres bien tassés de whisky. Sherwood Anderson et son amie Gertrude Stein qui tient salon à deux pas de là, au 27 rue de Fleurus, Ezra Pound qui tente de manipuler le cours de la poésie de langue anglaise, l'excentrique Nina Hamnett, émissaire du cercle du Bloomsbury,

James Joyce et Nora, à l'époque de la publication d'*Ulysse* par Sylvia Beach, le peintre anglais Augustus John, Ernest Hemingway, qui ne néglige aucun des lieux où la littérature et l'alcool font bon ménage, Henry Miller dont, comme le note Nino Frank, "les frénésies littéraires s'épanouissent au Sélect", tous ont donné ses lettres de noblesse à cet archipel anglo-saxon. Ce café a toujours été une terre d'asile pour les écrivains déracinés et assoiffés. Et, dans une moindre mesure, il l'est encore un peu aujourd'hui.

Pendant les Années folles, Montparnasse consacre son triomphe. Et la construction de *La Coupole* lui offre le temple le plus luxueux et le plus éblouissant. L'architecte Le Boucq dresse les plans d'un édifice de 1 600 m² abritant un café, une brasserie, un restaurant au premier étage, baptisé La Pergola, un dancing et un bar américain, désor-

Les fêtes de Montparnasse accompagnent les Années folles. Elles disparaissent avec la rapidité et l'inexorable montée de la crise européenne qui trouve son dénouement pathétique en 1939.

Ci-dessus : Bal en 1925 avec Foujita, Feder, Ladureau.

Page de gauche : Tsuguharu Foujita dans son atelier en 1957.

LE SELECT

mais indispensable pour attirer la clientèle anglophone. Les deux créateurs de cette basilique du parisianisme, Ernest Fraux, qu'on surnomme le "Citroën de la limonade", et René Lafon sont résolus à y attirer tout ce qui compte et a réussi dans le domaine de l'art, de la littérature et de la mode dans son acception la plus large. Car plus question ici de bohème : seuls ceux qui ont réussi peuvent être dignes de pénétrer dans cette magnifique machine à divertissement qui ne compte pas moins de quatre cent dix-huit employés. L'inauguration, en décembre 1927, est à la mesure de cette démesure. Le Tout-Paris y est convié et mille quatre cents bouteilles de champagne sont ouvertes pour fêter l'événement. Jean Cocteau, Pierre Benoit, Kisling, Foujita, Man Ray, Louis Aragon, Maurice Sachs, André Salmon, Maurice de Vlaminck, Henri Béraud, Blaise Cendrars, pour ne citer qu'eux, font partie des illustres invités, triés sur le volet, au baptême de ce paquebot de la notoriété.

Pour faire bonne figure et pour ancrer profondément *La Coupole* dans l'humus montparnassien, les patrons demandent à des artistes du cru d'en décorer les piliers. Par souci d'économie, ils se gardent bien de faire appel aux célébrités qui hantent déjà les lieux, bien que la rumeur a long-temps couru que Fernand Léger aurait concouru à cette entreprise. Ils choisissent des inconnus rémunérés avec quelques consommations gratuites. La machine est parfaitement au point et fonctionne vingt-quatre heures sur vingt-quatre. La vision quasi industrielle et tayloriste de leur mis-sion dans la sphère de la culture est une réus-site immédiate. C'est un va-et-vient ininter-rompu qui fascine Léon-Paul Fargue installé confortablement de l'autre côté du boule-vard, à la terrasse du *Sélect*, pour savourer le spectacle de ce qu'il appelle "ce Nijni-Novgorod en raccourci, cette fresque de soupeuses et de langoustes [...] de bohèmes sans linge et de *business men*, que rejetait chaque soir, dans le quatorzième arrondisse-ment, le simoun moderne".

Henry Miller a souvent préféré des cafés sans qualités comme ceux de Clichy, mais entre les deux guerres, il a néanmoins fréquenté Montparnasse, et notamment le Sélect, qui est une plaque tournante de la littérature de part et d'autre de l'Atlantique.

Les Américains se retrouvent au Sélect. Montparnasse et ses cafés, se situent à deux pas de l'appartement de Gertrude Stein (ci-dessus à gauche avec Alice Toklas) rue de Fleurus, lieu de pèlerinage de l'intelligentsia. Ernest Hemingway rend souvent visite à Sylvia Beach dans sa librairie de la rue de l'Odéon. Tous deux posent devant Shakespeare & Company en 1928. Hemingway vient de recevoir la lucarne de sa salle de bain sur la tête. Dans son roman *Paris est une fête*, Hemingway (ci-contre) raconte sa vie parisienne rythmée par de fréquentes visites dans les cafés qui y tiennent un rôle essentiel et où il rencontre régulièrement Francis Scott Fitzgerald (ci-contre, à droite).

Man Ray, figure légendaire
de Montparnasse,
dans son atelier de la rue
Campagne-Première.

Si l'on fait exception des surréalistes proches d'André Breton, il n'est pas âme qui vive dans le microcosme de la création de l'entre-deux-guerres à ne pas se mêler à la foule des habitués un moment ou à un autre de la journée. René Crevel et Robert Desnos, Curzio Malaparte et Salvador Dali, Max Jacob et Giorgio De Chirico, qui a son atelier rue Brown-Séquart, Antonin Artaud, Florent Fels, le directeur de la revue *L'Art vivant*, Louis Aragon, qui y fait la connaissance de la belle danseuse viennoise Lena Amsel avant de tomber dans les rets d'Elsa Triolet, qui l'attend assise à une table près de l'entrée, Pablo Picasso, Man Ray, qui s'est entiché de la capiteuse Kiki, l'égérie très peu farouche de ce temple païen, sont en tête de l'affiche de la prestigieuse distribution de ce grand théâtre des apparences.

Mais ce qui va engendrer la véritable dimension de *La Coupole* est sans nul doute l'invraisemblable afflux d'étrangers, qui constituent des cercles nationaux, régionaux ou linguistiques, apparaissant comme autant d'ambassades improvisées. C'est ainsi que les Soviétiques ont leur table où l'on reconnaît Vladimir Maïakovski, Elsa Triolet, Serge Prokofiev, Serge Eisenstein. Les Américains ont aussi leur table, où l'on voit Scott Fitzgerald, George Gershwin, Alexander Calder, Man Ray, McAlmon, Eugene Jolas, le directeur de la revue *Transition*, Ernest Hemingway et, un peu à l'écart, les enfants terribles du Nouveau Monde, Henry Miller et Anaïs Nin, quand ils ne sont ni au *Viking* ni au *Sélect*. Il y a aussi la table des réfugiés venus de l'Europe centrale qui regroupe, autour d'Hermann Kesten, des personnages tels que Joseph Breitbach, Joseph Riwkin, Joseph Wittlin, la jeune et belle Suédoise Ester Riwkin et sa sœur, Eugenia Söderberg. Leur nombre augmente avec une régularité implacable à mesure que le national-socialisme et que les dictatures

Ci-dessus : Florent Fels, directeur de la revue *L'Art vivant*, et Jules Pascin.

Page de droite : La façade illuminée de La Coupole en 1928.

Ci-contre : Pilier de La Coupole décoré par Marie Vassilieff. On s'est longtemps interrogé sur les véritables auteurs des peintures ornant ces piliers. Les récentes recherches prouvent qu'il ne s'agit que d'artistes de second rang. Classés monuments historiques, ils n'en témoignent pas moins de l'esthétique de Montparnasse au lendemain de son âge d'or.

triomphent dans leurs pays respectifs.

Mais ces cercles sont loin d'être hermétiques. Des émissaires passent d'une table à l'autre, les associations les plus inattendues sont provoquées et, dans ce gigantesque hall de gare métaphysique, Hugo von Hofmannsthal, Thomas et Heinrich Mann, Ford Madox Ford, Luis Buñuel, Max Jacob, James Joyce presque aveugle, André Derain, Rappoport, Fred Uhlman, Lawrence Durrell, ont pu se croiser. On parle mille langues différentes dans une épiphanie fiévreuse sur les banquettes de cette manufacture des idées d'une Europe saisie par le trouble et l'angoisse, dans l'attente d'une catastrophe annoncée.

Il y a aussi des solitaires, comme Georges Simenon, présent tous les jours quand il écrit *La Tête d'un homme* et *Les Caves du Majestic* car le café lui offre un décor idéal à ses trames.

Bien que les grandes heures de Montparnasse soient lointaines, des groupes de peintres la choisissent pour y tenir leurs sessions comme *Cercle et Carré* et, par la suite, *Abstraction-Création*. Piet Mondrian, qui vit à Paris, Wassily Kandinsky, qui a abandonné le Bauhaus depuis longtemps, Robert et Sonia Delaunay, Lipchitz, Brancusi, Marcoussis, Ozenfant, Paul Vermet échangent leurs

Ci-dessus : La grande salle de La Coupole en 1927.

Ci-contre : Des Montparnos inaugurent une exposition de leurs œuvres à La Coupole.

Page de droite en haut : Un réveillon de la Saint-Sylvestre à La Coupole. Les soirées costumées sont très courues pendant les Années folles.

En bas : Les Montparnos à La Coupole caricaturés par Sem.

points de vue et définissent les orientations de la peinture géométrique et néoplasticienne.

Comme La Rotonde, La Coupole finit par être la proie des touristes, étant une des étapes obligées de l'agence Cook. Pendant l'Occupation, la Gestapo s'installe au premier étage. La vie reprend son droit à la Libération et les artistes reviennent, les écrivains aussi, moins nombreux, moins régulièrement.

Montparnasse est entré dans l'histoire. Et l'histoire fige tout. Un musée s'est ouvert à l'emplacement de l'atelier de Marie Vassilieff. Les cafés de ce que Miller désigne comme le "delta de Vénus" et Pascin le "pubis vérolé du monde" ont tenu leur rang dans la saga du XXᵉ siècle. Ils nous émeuvent car ils restent le livre d'or de cette aventure sans égal.

MONTPARNASSE DE

Habiter Montparnasse : un rêve de provincial. Si d'autres essaient d'y retrouver des souvenirs d'enfance, moi j'essaye simplement de sentir l'âme de tous les grands artistes qui ont fréquenté Montparnasse. J'aime un quartier qui commencerait au Dôme, véritable figure de proue qui se dresse tel un navire bourgeois, irait jusqu'à la Closerie des Lilas pour se terminer au Sélect en passant par la rue Notre-Dame-des-Champs. Avec pour jardin le petit Luxembourg. Un triangle d'or dans lequel on ne se perd jamais. Les autocars n'y viennent jamais : pas de Sacré-Cœur, de Notre-Dame à visiter. L'âme de Boris Vian, Cocteau, Picasso n'est pas photographiable. Le passé de Montparnasse est dans la souvenance de tous ces peintres ou écrivains. C'est un peu comme le sourire du chat de Lewis Carroll : quand le chat n'est plus là, le sourire reste. Garants de cette âme, les cafés, les brasseries. Merci au Sélect, à la Rotonde, au Dôme de

PATRICE LECONTE

NE PAS AVOIR CHANGÉ. Y FLOTTENT DES SOUVENIRS DE CHAT. LES "PURISTES" ONT FUI LA COUPOLE. MOI J'Y SUIS RESTÉ FIDÈLE. IL Y A EU DES TRAVAUX. ET ALORS ? NE VA-T-ON PLUS À L'OLYMPIA PARCE QUE LE MUSIC-HALL S'EST FAIT LIFTER ? J'AI MES HABITUDES. LA ROTONDE EST EN FACE DE CHEZ MOI : J'AIME Y DONNER MES RENDEZ-VOUS. JE M'Y SENS CHEZ MOI. JE VAIS PARFOIS AU SÉLECT. J'AIME CE LIEU BOURRÉ D'AUTEURS AVEC DES SCÉNARIOS QU'ILS NE TOURNERONT JAMAIS. J'HABITE LE QUARTIER DEPUIS 15 ANS. J'AI DÉMÉNAGÉ UNE FOIS : JE SUIS PASSÉ DU 6^I DROITE AU 6^I GAUCHE. RIEN DE PLUS FORMIDABLE QUE DE DÉMÉNAGER DE LA SORTE. JE CONNAIS CHAQUE RECOIN DE CE QUARTIER. J'AIME CE QUARTIER POUR LES GENS QUI LE FRÉQUENTENT : MES AMIS D'ABORD QUE JE CROISE AU SÉLECT OU À LA ROTONDE. ET PUIS LES INCONNUS COMME CE PEINTRE DE RUE TOUJOURS HABILLÉ EN BLANC AVEC SA GRANDE BARBE ET QUI PEINT, TRÈS MAL D'AILLEURS, LE CAFÉ VAVIN ET LA ROTONDE. IL A DÛ PEINDRE CETTE DERNIÈRE AU MOINS 350 FOIS...

Ce soir-là nous étions assis à la terrasse de la Closerie et regardions la nuit tomber et les gens passer sur le trottoir et la lumière grise du soir changer, les deux whisky-sodas que nous bûmes n'exercèrent pas d'effets chimiques sur Scott. Je les guettais soigneusement pourtant, mais ils ne se produisirent pas, et Scott ne me posa pas de questions éhontées, ne fit rien d'embarrassant, ne prononça pas de discours et se conduisit comme un être normal, intelligent et charmant.

Ernest Hemingway

Un soir de 1913, à La Closerie, Apollinaire nous présenta Herwarth Walden, juif allemand, rédacteur d'une petite revue intitulée Der Sturm et dont la ressemblance avec Voltaire faisait dire à Guillaume beaucoup de choses drôles sur la postérité illégitime que l'auteur de Candide avait laissée en Prusse. Je me rappelle que lorsque Walden aborda Paul Fort, celui-ci tenait une oie dans les bras. D'où venait cette oie ? Cela ne pouvait être que celle qui, chez Paul Léautaud, montait sur la table au dessert. "Pourquoi, à Paris, dépose-t-on les lettres dans les becs de gaz ?" me demanda le directeur du Sturm.

André Billy

Les habitués du Dôme et de La Rotonde ne venaient jamais à La Closerie. Ils n'y trouvaient aucun de connaissance et nul n'aurait levé les yeux sur eux s'ils étaient venus. En ces temps-là, beaucoup de gens fréquentaient le carrefour Montparnasse-Raspail pour y être vu, et, dans un certain sens, ces endroits jouaient le rôle aujourd'hui dévolu aux "commères" des journaux chargées de distribuer chaque jour des succédanés quotidiens de l'immortalité.

Ernest Hemingway

Le Dôme, c'est un café du carrefour
Raspail-Montparnasse. Les
"Dômiers" ce sont les peintres
allemands qui le fréquentent. C'est
ici que se décidait l'admiration que
l'on professait en Allemagne pour tel
ou tel peintre français.

Guillaume Apollinaire

LE SELECT

C'est [au Sélect] que j'ai rencontré
Ernest Hemingway, Hart Crane,
E.E. Cummings... Ezra Pound, qui avait
conseillé à Joyce de me voir, me présenta
d'autres amis, Faulkner, sauvage et solitaire,
Wolfe, aussi sauvage et grand écrivain,
Farrell... Et Sherwood Anderson,
Bromfield, déjà célèbre, et bien sûr Crosby,
couvert de dollars et toujours généreux.

Philippe Soupault

De quelque façon qu'on le prît, nous étions toujours pauvres et je faisais encore de petites économies en prétendant, par exemple, que j'étais invité à déjeuner, pour me promener pendant deux heures au Luxembourg et décrire, au retour, mon merveilleux déjeuner à ma femme. Quand vous avez vingt-cinq ans et que vous appartenez à la catégorie des poids lourds, vous avez très faim lorsque vous sautez un repas. Mais cela aiguise aussi toutes vos perceptions… […] Je revenais maintenant sur mes pas, après être passé devant le Sélect …

Ernest Hemingway

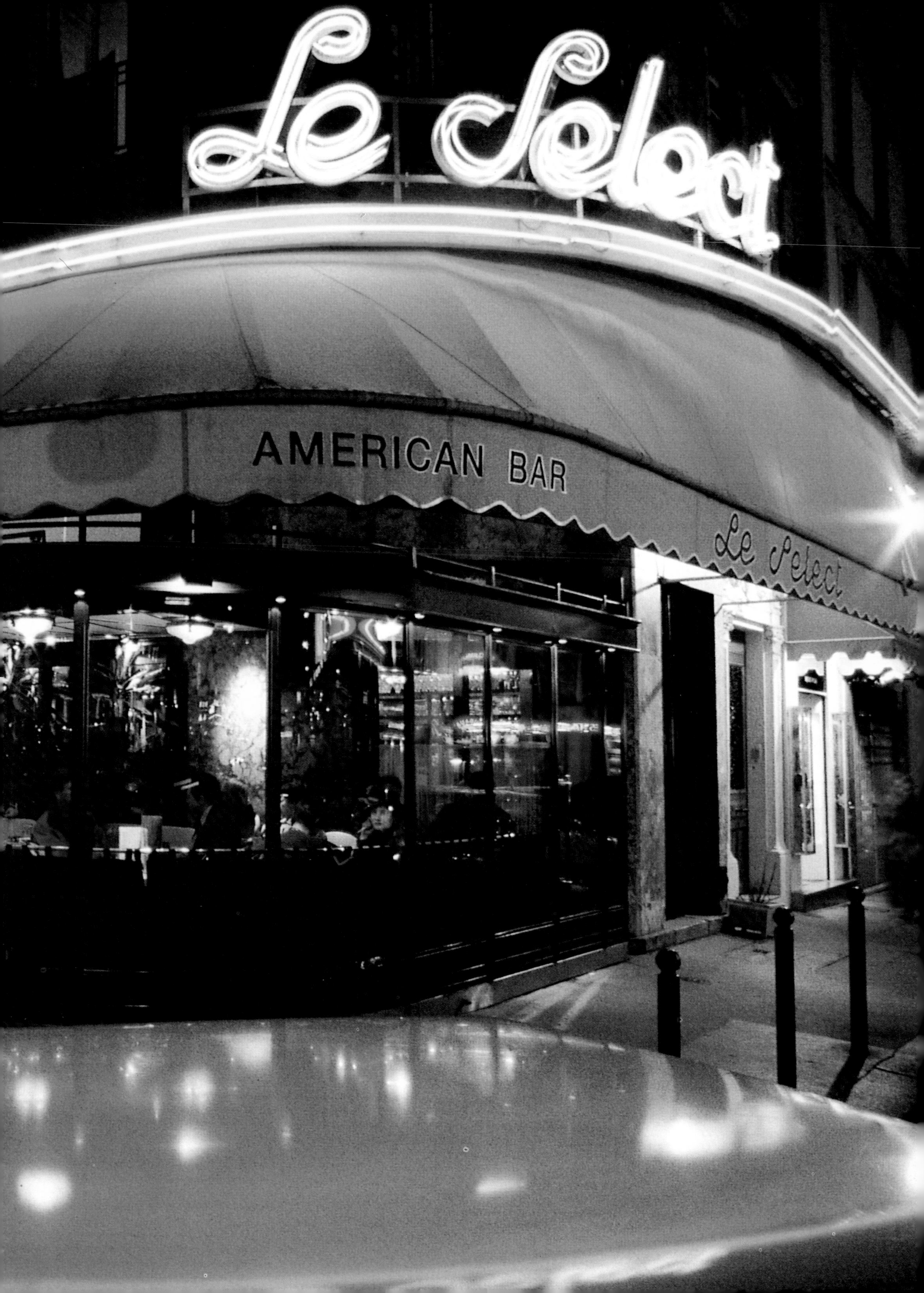
Le Select
AMERICAN BAR
Le Select

LA COUPOLE

À partir de ce jour, Yves [Klein] et moi deviendrons inséparables. Nous nous retrouvions tous les soirs à La Coupole où nous serons rejoints par les autres peintres. La Coupole était le haut lieu de la peinture internationale, peintres et sculpteurs s'y retrouvaient. Giacometti en était le point de mire ; les jeunes affluaient de toutes parts pour rencontrer le maître.

Iris Clert

Dîner avec les Salmon. Rencontre avec Friesz. On est allés à La Coupole. Kisling me
cherchant m'a trouvé… Man Ray, Kiki… Desnos… c'était gentil et gai. À un moment,
quand quelqu'un parlait de Derain, je disais : "En voilà un que je voudrais quand même
revoir avant de retourner en Amérique." Deux minutes après, voilà le Derain qui s'amène,
complètement saoul ! Je me suis bien amusé.

Jules Pascin

Comme tout le monde je me suis saoulé à La Coupole. Je débarquais pour
la première fois à Paris. Et depuis la terrasse, je voyais passer tous mes
héros – j'étais jeune… Avec Anaïs Nin, Miller et Pérlès, nous étions les
trois mousquetaires de La Coupole. On peut dire que Pérlès y dormait
presque. Quant à Anaïs Nin, elle se bagarrait au bar avec ses amants et
ses éditeurs. Elle aimait beaucoup les hommes.

Laurence Durrell

Fred, Henry, d'autres amis et moi au café, occupés à parler, à discuter, à contester, à raconter des histoires, jusqu'au moment où, dans la nuit, les réverbères s'éteignirent, la nuit se dissipa et une aube blafarde, timide, couleur terre de Sienne, entra par la fenêtre. L'aube ! L'aube, répétais-je.

Anaïs Nin

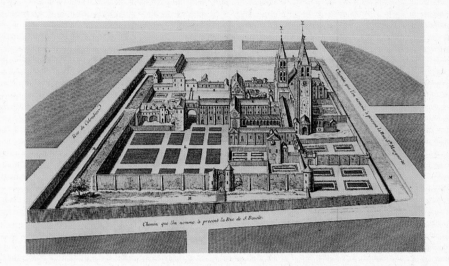

HIER ...

L'histoire de Saint-Germain-des-Prés, je veux bien entendu parler de son histoire dans la vie intellectuelle de Paris, aurait pu s'arrêter le 13 février 1790. Ce jour-là, l'Assemblée nationale abolit tous les ordres monastiques. Les cinq-six religieux qui résident dans la vieille abbaye l'abandonnent peu à peu. L'église est dévastée. Et, en 1794, un violent incendie causé par l'explosion d'un dépôt de munitions détruit une grande partie de l'inestimable bibliothèque. Ce qui a pu être sauvé des cinquante mille volumes et des quelque sept mille incunables est transporté à la Bibliothèque nationale.

La création de la petite église de la paroisse à l'époque mérovingienne ne pouvait pas laisser présager de l'essor de l'abbaye bénédictine, avec son bourg, ses terres de culture et d'élevage, ses fortifications, ses trois tours et surtout son incorporation à l'Université sous Philippe Auguste, contri-buant à faire de Paris l'un des plus grands centres de l'Europe médiévale.

En 1513, Guillaume Briçonnet réforme l'ordre régit par la règle de saint Benoît et s'attache à une renaissance de l'activité intellectuelle du monastère. Il rassemble une bibliothèque conséquente et y développe les sciences auxiliaires de l'histoire : la paléographie, l'historiographie et la connaissance patristique. Ses successeurs, Dom Dubreuil, Mabillon et Montfaucon poursuivent son œuvre. La Contre-Réforme est un aiguillon puissant pour l'épanouissement de ces études menées avec sérieux et constance.

Sur ces entrefaites, le bourg Saint-Germain a pris de l'ampleur et est devenu prospère. Une foire y a été créée après la mort de Charlemagne et Louis VII, par une charte au XIIe siècle, en assure la pérennité. Au début du XVIe siècle, on bâtit sur son emplacement une grande et belle halle per-

Page de gauche : En 1762, la Foire Saint-Germain est la proie d'un puissant incendie.

Ci-dessus : L'Abbaye de Saint-Germain-des-Prés avant 1640. Cette abbaye a été l'un des plus grands pôles intellectuels et aussi un des centres d'études très important au XVIIe siècle.

Pages précédentes : La place Saint-Germain-des-Prés en 1950. Le triangle d'or du carrefour où deux cafés, le Café de Flore et Les Deux Magots, régentent le microcosme de l'édition et des galeries d'art.

mettant d'abriter plus de trois cents loges pour des marchands forains. Tous les ans, quinze jours après Pâques, en plein Carnaval, la foire connaît une affluence immense. On y vend de tout, sauf des armes et des livres. À partir de 1726, il devient un marché permanent. La prostitution y a libre cours et les dames de l'aristocratie y rencontrent en secret leurs amants. On y joue aux boules ou aux quilles. On s'attroupe pour voir les ours danser et les bêtes féroces. On se divertit devant le castellet des montreurs de marionnettes. Des acteurs s'y produisent avec

grand succès, à tel point que le roi les fait jouer à la cour. Ils obtiennent même de représenter deux opéras. C'est en tout cas dans les allées de ce marché qu'un négociant arménien nommé Pascal loue une petite boutique qui a l'aspect d'un kiosque oriental pour proposer au chaland une boisson noirâtre et amère venue de l'Arabie heureuse encore bien peu prisée…

Le théâtre joue aussi un rôle considérable dans l'histoire de ce quartier de Paris. Le théâtre Guénégaud sert à partir de 1675 d'asile à la troupe de La Grange, directeur du Marais. Puis le roi, soucieux d'avoir un contrôle plus absolu sur les artistes décide la fusion de la troupe de l'Hôtel de Bourgogne et celle du théâtre du Faubourg Saint-Germain avec la compagnie de Molière. Ce nouveau théâtre cherche un lieu où s'installer pendant huit mois. En vain. On trouve enfin le jeu de paume de l'Étoile dans l'actuelle rue de l'Ancienne-Comédie. C'est en face de cet endroit livré au drame et à la farce que décide de s'installer un jeune Sicilien appelé Francesco Procopio dei Coltelli pour ouvrir une

maison de café. Il en fait rapidement le quartier général de la Comédie. L'endroit est assez accueillant et agréablement aménagé pour attirer la clientèle du théâtre, des fermiers généraux et des petits maîtres ainsi que les auteurs dramatiques, les comédiens et les premiers gazetiers et folliculaires. Ce "terrain neutre" est néanmoins un excellent forum pour les joutes verbales et les débats contradictoires. Jean de La Fontaine et Gresset l'auteur de *Vert Vert*, Danchet, le grammairien, Regnard, Crébillon Père et Fils figurent parmi ses hôtes assidus. Quand le fils de Procope,

Alexandre, prend la relève, le café est devenu le centre incontesté de la vie littéraire. Alexandre se prétend à la fois médecin et auteur dramatique, chansonnier et poète. Il fait tout en son pouvoir pour que son établissement conserve sa réputation. Il y attire Jean-Baptiste Rousseau, Houdar de La Motte, Fontenelle et puis Grimm, Lesage et une cohorte de nouvellistes en quête des derniers échos. *Le Procope* est vraiment le café des Lumières. Si on y voit fort peu Jean-Jacques Rousseau et Denis Diderot, contrairement à la légende, Voltaire y vient

Ci-contre : Annonce d'un banquet au Procope en 1895 par Le Comité de la "Vie de Bohème".

déguisé pour écouter les réactions provoquées par ses pièces, en particulier lors de la violente polémique avec Fréron qui a écrit une pièce satirique, *Les Philosophes*, à laquelle ce premier réplique quelques mois plus tard avec *L'Écosaisse ou Le Café*, dont l'action se déroule justement dans

Au XIXᵉ siècle, c'est sur la rive droite que s'installent les grands cafés à proximité de la Bourse, des banques, des agents de change, des rédactions des grands journaux et des revues influentes. Sur la rive gauche, la bohème fait cause commune avec le monde estudiantin au Quartier latin.

Le Procope au XVIIIᵉ siècle. Une légende persistante fait du Procope le café des Encyclopédistes. Mais il a néanmoins été le haut lieu des Lumières et l'antichambre de la Révolution française. Grimm, Danton ou Marat, notamment, s'y rassemblaient.

la salle du bon Procope. Et, pendant la Révolution, c'est le lieu de réunion de Danton, de Fabre d'Églantine et du Club des Cordeliers, de Marat et d'Hébert, où l'on célèbre en grande pompe la mort de Benjamin Franklin. Rebaptisé Café Zoppi pendant ces événements décisifs, il s'assoupit sous l'Empire. Les débuts du romantisme lui redonnent un peu de lustre, avec Alfred de Musset, Théophile Gautier et Victor Hugo l'année de la *Querelle d'Hernani*. Puis il retombe dans une profonde somnolence.

Un certain Théo de Bellefonds a l'intention de ressusciter le *Café Procope*. Il restaure et complète la bibliothèque de Zoppi, installe un petit théâtre et imprime une feuille. Des cafés connaissent des fortunes diverses autour de l'Odéon, tel le Café Voltaire, où Gino Severini a célébré ses épousailles avec Jeanne, la fille de Paul Fort, le François Iᵉʳ près du carrefour Buci, où Léon-Paul Fargue voit Paul Verlaine, quand il n'est pas au Procope ou ailleurs, car il n'est pas un lieu dans le quartier qui ne l'ait pas vu succomber à la tentation de la fée verte. Le fau-

bourg Saint-Germain est alors un coin paisible d'où semble s'être abstrait les agitations de la politique ou les affres de la création. Le Café Caron, rue des Saints-Pères, que fréquente Remy de Gourmont, est un havre paisible pour les retraités où l'on bavarde à mi-voix et évite les jeux bruyants. Huysmans le perçoit comme le parangon du café d'antan, à l'abri des injures du temps, des bouleversements de la vie moderne, quasiment immuable dans ses us et coutumes.

Toutefois, ces rues paisibles attirent les libraires, les éditeurs, les rédactions des revues sérieuses. *La Revue des Deux Mondes* de Buloz s'installe rue des Beaux-Arts au début des années 1830 et emploie des hommes nouveaux comme Alfred de Musset, Jules Simon ou Alexandre Dumas pour devenir la référence incontournable de son époque. La Librairie de "l'Histoire contemporaine" dirigée par Anatole-François Thibault, dit le Père France, est l'un des lieux fréquentés par les érudits du milieu du siècle dernier d'abord quai Malaquais, puis quai Voltaire, alors que les gens de lettres stationnent dans la librairie Honoré Champion, elle aussi sise quai Malaquais à partir de 1874. Henri Plon

rachète en 1854 l'Hôtel de Sourdéac rue Garancière et devient l'imprimeur de l'empereur. Le Cercle de la Librairie choisit pour siège l'ancien hôtel construit par Charles Garnier en 1879 et commence la publication de la Bibliographie de France. Au début de

La balustrade du Procope est classée.

notre siècle, ce sont les revues comme *Vers et Prose, Le Mercure de France* de Valette et Rachilde, qui est domiciliée rue de Condé ou la *NRF* d'André Gide et Jacques Rivière

Ci-dessus : Dans la salle du premier étage du café de Flore Charles Maurras crée le mouvement *Action française*. Il écrit plus tard un livre de souvenirs littéraires intitulé *Au signe de Flore*.

Ci-contre : Au Flore, dans les années 30, André Malraux s'installe toujours à la même place, près de la vitre, et commande un Pernod bien glacé.

boulevard tracé par le baron Haussmann. Il doit son nom charmant à une statue de la petite divinité qu'on dit s'être dressée de l'autre côté de boulevard. Après la fermeture

d'abord consignée dans l'arrière-boutique d'un teinturier de la rue Saint-Benoît, qui élisent les deux rives du boulevard Saint-Germain. Le caractère de l'ancien faubourg se fait imperceptiblement littéraire avant de devenir le pôle exclusif de l'édition française.

Le Café de Flore voit le jour en 1885, construit sur l'emplacement de l'ancienne abbaye, après l'achèvement du nouveau

du modeste Café Caron, ses clients s'y acclimatent et viennent y lire en paix leurs journaux. Remy de Gourmont y retrouve la même tranquillité. Les choses commencent à changer quand, après les convulsions de l'affaire Dreyfus, les jeunes monarchistes, rassemblés autour de Charles Maurras, son théoricien, y fondent l'*Action française* au premier étage. C'est là qu'il lance son

LES SOIRÉES DE PARIS

278, Bd Raspail, 278

Tél.: Saxe 55-43

DIRECTEURS:

GUILLAUME APOLLINAIRE ET JEAN CÉRUSSE

ABONNEMENTS

EDITION SIMPLE : FRANCE 10 FRS. ETRANGER 12 FRS
SUR HOLLANDE.. „ 25 „ „ 30 „

LE NUMÉRO: FRANCE 0,75 C. ETRANGER 0,90 C.

Paris, le _____ 191

Deux places de la part de Madame Apollinaire

Jacqueline Apollinaire

Guillaume Apollinaire, qui habite boulevard Saint-Germain, a ses habitudes au Flore. En 1911, il en fait la salle de rédaction pour sa revue *Les Soirées de Paris* créée avec Rouveyre, Billy et Salmon. Dès lors ce sera son bureau où il reçoit à heures fixes avec élégance. Ci-contre, avant sa mort en 1918.

Apollinaire présente André Breton (ci-contre en 1913) à Philippe Soupault en 1917 en disant : "Il faut que vous deveniez amis". En provoquant également la rencontre des deux jeunes hommes avec Aragon, Apollinaire jette les fondements du groupe surréaliste à Paris.

fameux appel à Henri d'Orléans, là que "le fait exprès des destins voulut que, sous le signe et la protection de cette déesse du Printemps, fussent élevées les premières et bien bruyantes rumeurs de notre Action française..." L'événement est assez retentissant pour attirer la curiosité de fins lettrés comme Maurice Barrès et Paul Bourget. C'est ainsi que peu à peu, la littérature s'installe dans le décor gris et crasseux du Flore. Guillaume Apollinaire l'adopte pour y rencontrer ses amis parce qu'il est encore en dehors des grandes routes de l'esprit parisien. Il y retrouve les poètes André Salmon et André Rouveyre, pour créer la revue *Les Soirées de Paris*. Jusqu'à la guerre, l'auteur d'*Alcools* règne en maître à la terrasse du Flore tous les mardis. Et quand il abandonne ses canons lorsqu'une permission lui est accordée, il quitte son petit appartement du boulevard pour rameuter ses vieux camarades autour de sa table et introniser les nouveaux venus. C'est ainsi que, sous son égide, Philippe Soupault fait la connaissance d'André Breton au cours du printemps 1917. Il favorise ensuite la rencontre de ces deux apprentis poètes avec Louis Aragon en cette même année où il invente le mot surréalisme.

La Grande Guerre terminée et Apollinaire tué par la grippe espagnole, la réputation du Café de Flore est solidement établie. Tristan Tzara, à peine arrivé de Zurich, y convoque les assises de dada. Non loin de ce clan turbulent, l'érudit Henri Martineau, directeur de la revue *Le*

1943. Une réunion au Flore autour de Jean-Paul Sartre. De gauche à droite : Raymond Bussières, Maurice Baquet, Marianne Hardy, Annette Poivre et Sartre. À partir de 1942, Sartre et Simone de Beauvoir se rendent quotidiennement au Flore pour travailler. Sartre y invente la nouvelle philosophie existentialiste qui triomphera après la révolution de Mai 68 et affirme *"les chemins du Flore ont été pour moi Les Chemins de la liberté..."* Phrase reprise depuis en exergue sur tous les menus du café.

Divan, s'entretient avec les inconditionnels de Stendhal. Un peu plus tard, André Malraux y sirote son Pernod glacé alors que les Américaines émoustillées se laissent bercer par les mélodies distillées par un orchestre. Léon-Paul Fargue y passe deux heures par jour, avec une ponctualité sans faille. On y voit, dans un coin, Michel Leiris converser avec Raymond Queneau. Les surréalistes, qui détestent Montparnasse, y organisent leurs réunions. Même les victimes des excommunications de Breton y conservent leurs habitudes. Georges Bataille, Georges Ribemont-Dessaignes, Robert

Desnos, Roger Vitrac s'asseyent avec ostentation à une table voisine. Et, non loin d'eux, viennent parfois des écrivains qui ne partagent rien des idéaux révolutionnaires de ces derniers, comme Thierry Maulnier, André Chamson ou Robert Brasillach. Le poète anglais Stephen Spender scrute avec ironie les manies de ses homologues français. Les éditeurs font régulièrement un détour au Flore car c'est le meilleur observatoire de l'activité littéraire.

Des artistes n'ont pas peur de se jeter dans ce chaudron de sorcières. Les frères Giacometti font ici leurs premiers pas dans le champ de

mine de l'art moderne, alors qu'André Derain, Pablo Picasso, le sculpteur Zadkine, qui ont derrière d'eux bien des batailles, affirment leur qualité d'anciens combattants de l'art fauve ou cubiste.

Le théâtre trouve lui aussi son foyer au rez-de-chaussée. Jean-Louis Barrault, Roger Blin, Sylvia Bataille et la joyeuse bande du groupe Octobre dirigée par le cinéaste Jean-Paul Le Chanois, débarquent en faisant grand tapage.

La drôle de guerre, puis la moins drôle campagne de France et l'armistice vident le café de son petit monde turbulent. Simone de Beauvoir comprend vite le parti qu'elle peut tirer de cet endroit solitaire et bien chauffé qui lui procure un sentiment d'intimité : elle en fait son bureau. Jean-Paul Sartre l'imite au début de 1942 et voilà le café transformé en la fabrique de *L'Être et le Néant*. Petit à petit tous ceux que les événements avaient éloignés

reviennent prendre leur rang dans ce petit théâtre discret. De nouvelles têtes apparaissent, comme Simone Signoret, alors qu'à Nice, Yves Allégret tourne *La Boîte aux rêves*, un film où il reconstitue le décor de l'établissement parisien dans ses moindres détails.

Après la Libération, à cause de la mode foudroyante de l'existentialisme, Sartre et Beauvoir désertent le Flore : on le visite comme le musée Grévin. Quoi qu'il en soit, les écrivains anglo-saxons, dont la majeure partie est membre du P.C.F. (le Pouilly Club de France), lui sont fidèles. Truman Capote, Lawrence Durrell, Ernest Hemingway ne le boudent pas. Et des anciens comme Francis Carco, Raymond Carco, Marcel Achard, Pierre Mac Orlan y reviennent parfois. Même Sartre le fréquente encore accompagné par Maurice Merleau-Ponty et Albert Camus ne le dédaigne pas. Pablo Picasso s'installe le soir en face de

La terrasse du Flore
en 1964 réunit un grand
nombre de talents.
De gauche à droite :
Bernard Lucas fondateur
du Tabou, Daniel Filipacchi,
Victor Trauner, Maurice
Casanova (propriétaire du
Bilboquet), Paul Boubal le
patron du Flore. Au premier
plan : Guy Béart, Jean-
Claude Merle fondateur
de la discothèque devenue
le Bilboquet, Georges
et André Beller (deux des
frères Jacques), Jean Cau,
Pierre Prévert et
Daniel Gélin.

Juliette Gréco est un personnage phare de Saint-Germain-des-Prés. Ci-dessous : assise sur les marches de l'église Saint-Germain-des-Près en compagnie d'Anne-Marie Cazalis, inséparable amie dans cette après-guerre libératrice à Saint-Germain.

Dans les années cinquante, elle est une muse du Tabou, l'une des plus célèbres caves du quartier où l'on vient écouter Charlie Parker, Miles Davis, etc. En haut Sidney Bechet et Claude Luther.

l'entrée entouré d'amis espagnols. Salvador Dali y distille ses extravagances. Et Antonin Artaud y fait une dernière apparition avant de mourir. Le milieu du cinéma et celui du théâtre l'envahissent : Gérard Philipe et Brigitte Bardot, Roman Polanski et Jean Rouch, Joseph Losey et Astruc comptent parmi ses *aficionados*. Cela n'empêche nullement Jacques Lacan d'y faire son entrée tous les jours et Roland Barthes d'y passer quelques quarts d'heure le matin.

L'histoire du *Café des Deux Magots* a une préhistoire : un magasin de nouveautés créé dans la rue de Buci en 1813, ensuite transféré rue de Rennes en 1873, lui a donné son nom qu'il devait à une pièce à succès de

Marcel Servrin, *Les Deux Magots de la Chine*, et lui a laissé ces deux belles sculptures en bois avec les sages mandarins chinois. Quand il ouvre ses portes en 1891, il est fréquenté par des comédiens et une poignée de financiers. Oscar Wilde vient y traîner sa solitude et l'amertume de son exil alors que des écrivains comme Léon Daudet, Rosny Aîné l'adoptent. Quelques transfuges de Montparnasse forment le premier cercle d'habitués. André Derain explique sa théorie des cubes à la terrasse à André Salmon. Et on raconte qu'Alfred Jarry y est entré pour déclarer sa flamme à une jeune dame en tirant un coup de revolver dans la vitre, histoire de rompre la glace. Quand

En 1813, les Deux Magots, proposent aux élégantes Parisiennes un grand choix de nouveautés. Né à l'angle des rues de Seine et de Buci, le magasin est tranféré à l'angle de la rue de Rennes en 1873. Il disparaît en 1881 pour être remplacé dans un premier temps par le service d'expédition des Grands Magasins du Printemps, puis par des marchands de vins en 1884 et enfin, sept ans plus tard, par le café.

1898. Alfred Jarry, le bohème impénitent, le père d'Ubu, parcourt à vélo le trajet qui sépare sa maison de Corbeil, dans la banlieue parisienne, de Paris où il retrouve ses amis aux Deux Magots.

Guillaume Apollinaire est soupçonné en 1912 d'avoir dérobé des statuettes phéniciennes au Louvre, ses fidèles compagnons y tiennent assemblée. Peu de temps après, le petit groupe fonde la revue *Les Soirées de Paris*. La création du théâtre du Vieux-Colombier en 1913 y amène Jacques Copeau et sa troupe. Et bientôt Paul Léautaud et l'équipe du *Mercure de France* au grand complet l'adoptent.

Immédiatement après la guerre, André Breton, qui déteste le charivari de Montparnasse, compose avec soin le cercle d'amis qui va constituer le mouvement surréaliste. Louis Aragon, René Crevel, Paul Éluard, Robert Desnos l'y retrouvent pour mener les premières expériences dont rend compte la revue *Littérature*. Des ukases sont promulgués sans ménagement et des expéditions punitives sont préméditées autour de leur table

attitrée. Montparnasse ne tarde cependant pas à annexer ce séjour encore préservé. À la fin des années vingt, le café est le haut lieu de l'intelligentsia parisienne. Les groupes pullulent à sa terrasse et on peut y distinguer Le Corbusier ou Roland Dorgelès, Jean Tardieu ou Maurice Sachs, Robert Denoël ou Audiberti, Antonin Artaud ou Chardonne. Jean Giraudoux, qui travaille au ministère des Affaires étrangères, a sa propre table. Saint-Exupéry arrive en compagnie de sa secrétaire, Françoise Giroud à l'époque où il écrit *Courrier-Sud*. Pablo Picasso y fait la connaissance d'une belle jeune femme, Dora Maar. Les étrangers se jettent sans attendre dans cette mêlée : James Joyce s'entoure du clan de ses sectateurs, Bertold Brecht, Alfred Döblin, Stefan Zweig, Robert Musil, Anna Seghers, Heinrich Mann, Ernst

Weiss, le grand journaliste tchèque Egon Erwin Kisch, Joseph Roth, et tant d'autres exilés venus de l'Europe entière forment un fascinant tableau littéraire qui ne cesse de se reformuler.

De nouvelles revues y voient le jour, comme *Bifur*, dirigée par Georges Ribemont-Dessaignes et Nino Frank et *La Courte Paille* créée par Henri Philippon. Les mondes les plus divers et les plus éloignés se croisent et se heurtent sous le regard impénétrable des deux dignitaires de la Chine ancienne : Henri Michaux a pu rencontrer Francis Carco dans ce grand carrefour des opinions et des écoles littéraires, des engagements et des groupes artistiques.

Le démon de la politique saisit les Deux Magots au cours des années trente. Les participants du Congrès International pour la Défense de la Culture, qui se tient à la Mutua-

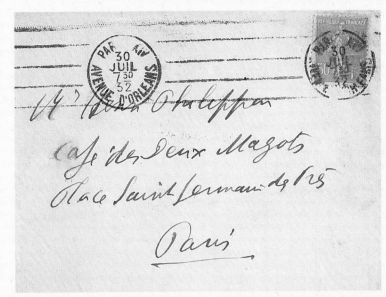

lité en 1935, y poursuivent leurs sessions, Eugène Dabit et Aldous Huxley discutant vivement avec Bertold Brecht et Robert Musil. Les réunions de l'Union pour la Vérité, qui ont lieu rue de Rennes et auxquelles participent Paul Nizan, Romain Rolland et André Gide, s'achèvent presque toujours au café.

Ci-dessus : Lettre d'Antonin Artaud à Henri Philippon, créateur du prix des Deux Magots, envoyée en juillet 1932 directement au café. En sortant de l'asile de Rodez, Artaud aime monter sur les tables de café pour lire un poème érotique devant les clients stupéfaits.

Les Anglo-Saxons sont fidèles aux Deux Magots. *Ci-contre* : Ernest Hemingway et Janet Flanner, correspondante du *New Yorker*, pendant la Libération.

James Joyce est une figure familière des Deux Magots. Il y retrouve l'érudit Louis Gilet et y invite Hemingway à boire du sherry.

vaillent ou lisent en silence dans la salle à moitié déserte. À la Libération, Sartre et Beauvoir fuient le Café de Flore et se réfugient dans ce havre de paix. Mais bientôt les anciens habitués reviennent et la joyeuse bande des frères Prévert redonne vie à l'auguste maison alors que les surréalistes se réapproprient leur territoire après un long exil à New York. Boris Vian, Albert Camus et Violette Leduc comptent parmi les figures familières de cette phase nouvelle de cette histoire où s'installe le mythe de Saint-Germain-des-Prés dont Juliette Gréco est devenue la grande prêtresse.

À l'origine, la *Brasserie des Bords du Rhin*, fondée en 1877 par Léonard Lipp, est le théâtre d'une curieuse cérémonie : on y signe le Manifeste des Cinq contre la publication de *La Terre* d'Émile Zola. Très rapidement, l'endroit se peuple de personnages extrava-

La nouvelle guerre qui s'annonce met un terme à ces féroces festivités de l'intelligence. Tous rideaux tirés, ceux qui ont échappé à la fureur des événements tra-

En 1933 se réunit le jury du premier prix littéraire des Deux Magots (ci-contre) comprenant notamment Michel Leiris et Georges Bataille. Ce premier prix fut décerné à Raymond Queneau pour son roman *Le Chiendent*.

gants, comme quelques poètes dissidents du groupe des Hydropathes, des membres du groupe des Hirsurtes et une poignée de Décadents, dont Jean Moréas, quand il ne vaticine pas au Café Vachette, Laurent Tailhade et Paul Mounet. Marcel Proust, qui ne quitte pas volontiers l'hôtel Ritz, envoie la sœur de Céleste acheter de la bière chez le brave Alsacien. Alfred Jarry descend de bicyclette pour y prendre un repas à l'envers, c'est-à-dire en commençant par le dessert pour finir par l'entrée. Quand la guerre est déclarée avec l'Allemagne, Lipp retire le mot Rhin de son enseigne et ne le remet qu'une fois Strasbourg revenue dans le giron de la France en 1918.

Vers 1945, fuyant les admirateurs qui se pressent pour apercevoir le célèbre couple, Simone de Beauvoir et Jean-Paul Sartre désertent le Flore et s'installent fréquemment aux Deux Magots pour travailler en paix à deux petites tables voisines.

117

LES DEUX MAGOTS
SAINT-GERMAIN-DES-PRÉS

Le rendez-vous
de l'élite intellectuelle

L'établissement est racheté en 1920 par un homme arrivé de l'Aveyron, Marcellin Cazes. Il modifie son nom, le baptisant *Brasserie Lipp* en hommage à l'ancien propriétaire qui a su se faire une très bonne réputation. Un poète hors du commun se propose comme locataire à vie : Léon-Paul Fargue, l'auteur du *Piéton de Paris*. Il faut dire qu'il le connaît comme sa poche car son père et son oncle l'ont décoré de céramiques. Le succès est énorme. Sa clientèle provient des milieux les plus divers : des étudiants des Beaux-Arts, des rentiers, des hommes d'affaires, des commerçants du quartier, puis après dix-sept heures, des éditeurs voisins, des fonctionnaires venant des ministères du boulevard, des médecins, des bandes d'artistes, des journalistes en quête d'échos. Mais la caractéristique de Lipp est sans aucun doute d'attirer des hommes politiques, surtout les députés de province, qui y retrouvent l'aspect accueillant et pas bégueule des bistrots cossus et des brasseries chaleureuses de leurs villes ou de leurs bourgs d'origine. Il existe chez Lipp un côté "sous-préfecture" qui les rassure. Et la politique y règne en souveraine : on y compose des cabinets, on en défait d'autres. Des ministères sombrent. Des coalisions s'esquissent. Des alliances sont tra-

Page de droite en bas à gauche : 1967, Saint-Germain-des-Prés rend hommage à Marcel Carné et Jacques Prévert en présence notamment de Jean-Louis Barrault, Jacques Charrier, Michel Simon et Michèle Morgan.

Ci-dessus : L'atmosphère cosy des Deux Magots ne convient pas trop au turbulent Jacques Prévert (et vice versa !). Le poète et sa bande émigrent au Flore dans les années quarante.

Page de droite en bas à droite : Roland Barthes, directeur d'études à l'École des Hautes Études en sciences sociales et professeur au Collège de France, prend volontiers son petit déjeuner au Café de Flore.

Ci-dessus : René Saint Paul aux Deux Magots.

Ci-dessous : Gérard Philipe en 1959 à la terrasse des Deux Magots. Acteurs de théâtre et de cinéma adoptent le carrefour Saint-Germain dès les années trente.

hies. Les chefs de parti élaborent des stratégies et, parfois, on n'est pas loin de risquer l'affrontement violent. Par exemple, Léon Blum doit rebrousser chemin un soir de 1936, parce qu'une escouade de jeunes royalistes l'attend pour le bastonner. Ce genre d'incident n'est pas rare. Mais si la politique a ici ses droits et ses privilèges, elle coexiste avec le théâtre et le cinéma, la littérature et la création sous toutes ses formes. Des clients démontrent une assiduité rare, comme Colette ou Picasso, mais aussi André Gide, qui vient en solitaire, ou bien encore Robert Desnos accompagné de sa femme, Youki. Le prix Cazes, créé en 1935, en fait une annexe indispensable de l'univers du livre qui a définitivement pris racine dans les parages. Hemingway parachève de fabriquer la légende de

ce lieu unique dans son roman *Paris est une fête*.

La Seconde Guerre mondiale passe et la Brasserie Lipp retrouve ses fastes. Des têtes nouvelles font leur entrée. Michel Butor, à l'époque où il écrit le *Passage de Milan*, Daniel Boulanger, Patrick Waldberg, Jacques Laurent, qui en demeure le plus fidèle pilier, René de Solier, mais aussi des peintres et des sculpteurs comme Max Ernst, Giorgio De Chirico, Alberto Giacometti, Alexander Calder, Riopelle, Sam Francis, Joan Mitchell, et une pléiade de jeunes gens ambitieux heureux de côtoyer d'illustres aînés. Et l'édition n'est pas de reste : Georges Lambrichs, quand il travaille encore aux Éditions de Minuit, puis quand il dirige la collection "Le Chemin" chez Gallimard, Joachim Vital, qui y jette les fondations des Éditions de la Différence, ont leur table pour recevoir des auteurs de tous les horizons.

La brasserie Lipp dans les années trente. À cette époque, elle est plus que jamais le centre névralgique de la vie politique – parlementaires et ministres y sont nombreux – sans pour autant perdre son statut de refuge des arts et des lettres.

Jean-Jacques Brochier est persuadé que Lipp n'est plus Lipp depuis que Roger Cazes a disparu. Mais le quartier aussi s'est métamorphosé en profondeur, livré dans son intégralité à l'industrie de la mode. Et d'aucuns finissent par regretter l'horrible Drug-store parce qu'il n'y avait plus que lui pour témoigner des jours anciens où le triangle d'or du carrefour a attiré un microcosme foisonnant sur lequel a veillé longtemps la statue de Denis Diderot, qui avait un sourire bienveillant et moqueur.

Et pas moyen de trouver refuge dans l'abri souterrain du *Bar du Pont-Royal* car il est fermé depuis plusieurs années. Ce bar a été le centre névralgique de l'édition de la rive gauche. Situé à deux pas de Gallimard, de Denoël, de la galerie Maeght, pas très loin non plus de Fayard, de la Table Ronde, de Grasset et du Magazine littéraire, des Éditions de l'Herne, on a vu y descendre tous ceux qui ont compté dans la république des lettres, mais aussi des arts. Repaire de Gallimard et de René Julliard, de Fasquelle et de l'infatiguable Lambrichs, de Christian Bourgois et de Philippe Sollers, il a accueilli des poètes magnifiques comme Giuseppe Ungaretti et Jean Tardieu, des romanciers comme Romain Gary et Antoine Blondin et, au fond, quasiment tous ceux qui

Ci-dessus : Giorgio De Chririco devant chez Lipp.

Ci-contre : Alexander Calder chez Lipp.

ont publié dans ces maisons. Francis Bacon s'y est risqué volontiers quand il descendait à l'hôtel et Helène Delprat ou Marco Del Re y ont fait des incursions. Il va, dit-on, rouvrir ces prochains mois. Même si son univers s'y reconstitue peu ou prou, le Pont-Royal ne pourra plus être tel qu'en lui-même.

Oui, les temps changent et les visages changent. Ce qui fut ne sera plus et rien ne sert de cultiver trop de nostalgie. En revanche, la mémoire de ces années si riches et presque miraculeuses est un trésor précieux pour les générations futures. Et ceux qui liront ces vers de Bernard Delvaille sauront que d'un côté ou de l'autre du boulevard Saint-Germain se sont joués plusieurs actes décisifs de l'histoire de notre culture :

Jazz
7 heures du soir en hiver
à Saint-Germain-des-Prés
le seul endroit du monde où la vie soit possible
Comme un tigre dans la jungle
Jean Genet traîne sa solitude royale
et son orgueil
Le ciel flamboie
Les trottoirs sont mouillés
Dans les caves enfumées et chaudes
de la ville rouge et or
où la trompette se lamente
danses-tu
ou si seulement
tu tues le temps
Ainsi chaque soir
la vie te jette à la rue
et tu erres
de café en café
fumant cigarette sur cigarette
tordant les citrons glacés de la nuit.

Jacques et Pierre Prévert
à la Fontaine des Quatre-
Saisons. Les frères Prévert
appartiennent de droit
à la mythologie de Saint-
Germain-des-Prés. Ils y font
leur entrée pendant le
Front populaire, lorsqu'ils
collaborent au groupe
Octobre, une version très
française du théâtre d'*agit
prop* soviétique.

Saint-Germain de Juliette Gréco

C'est Hélène Duc qui m'avait fait connaître le Flore. Ma mère et ma sœur avaient été déportées. Moi, je sortais de Fresnes. On y trouvait des gens passionnants. Je me souviens surtout qu'il y faisait chaud. Sur chaque table, on trouvait une petite bouteille ronde contenant de la saccharine. On prenait grand soin de faire durer au minimum deux heures le temps de boire cette chose hautement improbable qui tenait lieu de café. À la Libération, le Flore devint un lieu de rendez-vous extraordinairement vivant. Il y avait là Prévert, la beauté fragile, mystérieuse et hiératique de Simone Signoret. Anne-Marie Casalis, Brienne, Maurice Baquet et tant d'autres. Et puis Sartre qui écrivait au premier étage la tête penchée et qui m'intimidait de son regard perçant. À se demander du reste qui il n'y avait pas. À ce panthéon des arts et des lettres se mêlaient des voyeurs élégants sur lesquels nous laissions planer notre ironie. Pour ma part quand on me demandait si j'étais bien Juliette Gréco, je répondais quelquefois : "En effet mon nom est Gréco... Cela s'écrit en cinq lettres." Est-ce la tradition dans le savoir-faire des garçons en service, à leur façon de vous reconnaître ? Au charme et à l'accueil très particulier de la caissière dont le sourire semble toujours vous signifier que vous êtes accepté au sein de cette famille bizarre ? L'endroit, quelle que soit l'époque a toujours fonctionné – et fonctionne toujours – comme un monde clos. Chose étrange, aucun des gens que je n'aime pas n'y vient jamais. Il s'établit une sorte de sélection naturelle qui fait barrage. Je suis toujours sûre d'y faire de bonnes rencontres. Si je suis pressée, je m'installe à l'intérieur dans un coin derrière la porte mais le plus souvent j'y viens déjeuner au premier étage. C'est là que j'y retrouve tous mes copains. Aujourd'hui à Saint-Germain-des-Prés les maisons de couture prennent le pas sur les librairies. Faute de goût inacceptable, on vient de détruire sans aucun respect pour le passé, l'ancien appartement de Marcel Carné, rue de l'Abbaye. Le quartier devient une sorte d'avenue Montaigne *bis*. Mais Dieu merci, le Flore reste le Flore et j'y reste plus que jamais fidèle.

Saint-Germain de Françoise Sagan

Quand j'ai commencé à fréquenter Saint-Germain-des-Prés, cela
faisait déjà dix ans que Jean-Paul Sartre, Boris Vian et Juliette Gréco
y tenaient le haut du pavé. De fait j'ai intégré l'univers du Flore
et des Deux Magots dans un parfait anonymat qui, timidité oblige,
me convenait plutôt. Pour tout vous dire, je préférais bien mieux
mes escapades "Aux Assassins", rue Saint-Benoît. Y manger des steaks
avec mes petits copains de dix-neuf ans (j'en avais tout juste dix-sept)
me semblait alors le comble de la débauche. Tout a commencé
à changer avec le succès impressionnant, pour moi, qu'obtint
mon premier roman *Bonjour Tristesse*. C'est aux Deux Magots
que je reçus ma première grande leçon de vie consécutive à cette
soudaine entrée sur la scène littéraire. Arthur Adamov, grand
homme de théâtre, vint m'emprunter de l'argent. Tandis que
je lui signais un chèque, il ajouta en guise de remerciement :
"Rassurez-vous, cet argent je ne vous le rendrai jamais, mais
croyez bien que je ne vous en voudrai jamais non plus." Sur le coup,
je n'ai pas compris. C'est bien plus tard que j'ai réalisé ce
qu'il avait voulu dire. En constatant à mon corps défendant
que nombre de tapeurs à qui j'avais prêté de l'argent changeaient
de trottoir en me croisant. Sans même que j'ai songé à leur parler
de leur dette. C'est cette réplique teintée d'humanité d'Adamov
qui m'a fait aimer Les Deux Magots. J'y viens régulièrement
et je m'installe en règle générale à l'extérieur ou en entrant à gauche.
En revanche, je n'ai jamais compris comment pouvait-on faire pour
y travailler. Personnellement je n'ai jamais pu écrire ne fût-ce qu'une
seule ligne au café. Ce truc-là, c'était bon pendant la guerre.
On manquait cruellement de chauffage et les gens se regroupaient
au café pour se réchauffer. Croyez-moi, après la Libération, Sartre
n'a plus écrit aucun livre au Flore. Il préférait tout comme moi,
être au calme, chez lui !

Les surréalistes avaient leur table
[…] face à la porte, d'où ils
pouvaient insulter à loisir un
quelconque nouvel arrivé ayant
eu maille à partir avec eux, ou dire
à haute voix leur intention de
cravacher un éditorialiste écrivant
dans un quelconque journal
antisurréaliste, pour avoir
mentionné leur nom ou, pire,
ne pas l'avoir mentionné.

Janet Flanner

Au café, dans le bruit des voix, la pleine lumière, les coudoiements,

Robert Desnos n'a qu'à fermer les yeux et il parle, et au milieu des bocks,

des soucoupes, tout l'océan s'écroule avec ses fracas prophétiques et ses

vapeurs ornées de longues oriflammes.

Louis Aragon

C'était Henri Michaux, pas encore Plume, mais rieur et déjà chauve,
qui nous rejoignait. Un matin au soleil glorieux, nous le vîmes
apparaître en compagnie d'un grand gaillard massif et timide, au petit
pif en l'air qu'il nous présenta non sans goguenardise, comme un nouve
héros de qui André Gide s'apprêtait à lancer le livre de début : ce fut
ma première rencontre avec Antoine de Saint-Exupéry.

Nino Frank

C'est ici que le surréalisme reprend ses droits. On vous donne un encrier qui se ferme avec un bouchon de champagne et vous voilà en train. Images, descendez comme des confettis : images, partout images.

Louis Aragon

Un jour je rencontrais Joyce qui se promenait sur le boulevard Saint-Germain. [...] Il m'invita à prendre un verre et nous allâmes aux Deux Magots où nous commandâmes deux sherry secs.

Ernest Hemingway

Des Deux Magots
je ne connaissais guère que
la terrasse incomparable,
la plus belle de Paris, face
à la vieille église [...].
Des écrivains, des artistes,
dont André Derain,
y coudoyaient des Anglais
et des Américains.
La clientèle anglo-saxonne
se composait surtout
d'esthètes, de cette espèce
arrivant tout droit de
Florence pour visiter
l'atelier de Delacroix, place
de Furstenberg [...]

André Salmon

Camus, je me rappelle l'avoir vu seul, parce que je sortais de chez ma mère et je descendais aux Deux Magots, le matin [...]

Jean-Paul Sartre

Nous avions choisi le Café de Flore parce
que nous étions sûrs d'y être moins dérangés
qu'ailleurs. Nous prîmes place à la première table
à gauche, entre la porte et l'escalier, le long
de la glace de la devanture.

Guillaume Apollinaire

Le soir [Picasso] s'asseyait toujours
à la seconde table, face à l'entrée
principale, en compagnie d'amis
espagnols [...] Il ne faisait rien si ce
n'est boire à petites gorgées une bouteille
d'eau minérale, bavarder avec ses amis
espagnols et étudier les gens qui
ne le regardaient pas directement.
Sa libation terminée, il rentrait
invariablement chez lui.

Janet Flanner

Café de Flore

Vers 1942, je vis arriver un monsieur qui venait de l'ouverture
jusqu'à midi et de l'après-midi jusqu'à la fermeture. Il venait
souvent avec une dame et ils se tenaient fréquemment éloignés l'un
de l'autre à des tables différentes, mais toujours dans le même coin
quand ils étaient en bas. Je suis resté longtemps sans savoir qui
c'était. L'après-midi, dans la salle du premier, on les voyait,
toujours avec un grand dossier, gratter d'interminables papiers.
Sartre fut mon plus mauvais client ! Il demeurait des heures
à gribouiller du papier devant une unique consommation.

Paul Boubal

146

Café de Flore

L'hiver surtout, je m'efforçais d'y arriver dès l'ouverture pour occuper la meilleure place, celle où il faisait le plus chaud, à côté du tuyau de poêle. J'aimais beaucoup le moment où dans la salle encore vide, Boubal, un tablier bleu noué autour des reins, ranimait son petit univers. Pendant une heure ou deux, il ne décolérait pas. D'une voix irritée, il donnait des ordres au plongeur qui, par une trappe ouverte près de la caisse, remontait des bouteilles et des boîtes [...] peu à peu Boubal se calmait ; il ôtait son tablier ; blonde, bouclée, rose, soignée, sa femme descendait à son tour l'escalier et s'installait à la caisse.

Simone de Beauvoir

Le Flore est tendu d'épais rideaux, et il
y a de nouvelles banquettes rouges, c'est
superbe. Maintenant, les cafés ont
appris à bien se camoufler, ils allument
toutes les lampes et on est saisi par cet
éclat quand on arrive de dehors.

Simone de Beauvoir

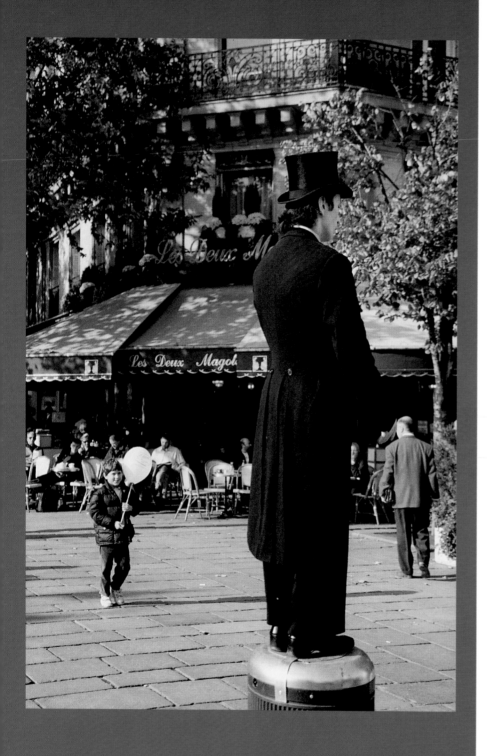

*Je ne sais plus quel humoriste
prétendait avec raison jadis
qu'on pourrait écrire une
histoire de la civilisation
en limitant l'étude de celle-ci
à celle des cafés.*

Léon-Paul Fargue

Il y a quelque trente ans, je suis entré
pour la première fois chez Lipp, brasserie
peu connue encore et que mon oncle
et mon père, ingénieurs spécialisés,
venaient de décorer de céramiques et
de mosaïques. À cette époque, tous les
céramistes faisaient à peu près la même
chose. Style manufacture de Sèvres,
Deck ou Sarreguemines. On ne se
distinguait entre artisans que par
la fabrication, les procédés d'émaillage
ou de cuisson, la glaçure plus ou moins
parfaite.

Léon-Paul Fargue

Dès lors, Lipp eut en fait trois
clientèles : à midi, des
hommes d'affaires, des
commerçants du quartier
qui voulaient déjeuner dans
un endroit calme et sérieux ;
de cinq à huit heures des
écrivains, libraires, éditeurs,
magistrats, fonctionnaires,
médecins, artistes qui se
réunissaient pour bavarder
ou se délasser de leurs travaux
devant des demis ou des
apéritifs ; et le soir, le Tout-
Paris.

Robert Cazes

*Chez Lipp, je bois, je mange,
j'écris, je regarde des visages
et cela dure déjà depuis très
longtemps.*

Jacques Laurent

RECE
DIS
CAFÉ
DEPA

RTES

RIS

SRIS

JBENNER
13 DEC. 62

Croque-Monsieur

Préchauffer le four en position grill à 220°C
Disposer le jambon, puis le fromage sur une tranche
de pain beurrée. Saler et poivrer. Saupoudrer le tout
avec le fromage râpé. Faire griller au four
quelques minutes. Lorsque le croque-monsieur
est doré et croustillant, le sortir du four
et servir immédiatement.

Ingrédients

1 tranche de pain de Poilâne
1 tranche de jambon de Paris
1 fine tranche d'emmenthal
1 cuillère à soupe d'emmenthal râpé
Beurre
Sel, poivre

Welsh rarebit

Ingrédients

150 g de cheddar
1 tranche de pain de mie toastée
1 trait de bière
Quelques gouttes de sauce anglaise

Dans une casserole faire fondre le fromage, mouiller avec la bière, fouetter jusqu'à l'obtention d'une pâte crémeuse. Disposer la tranche de pain légèrement humidifiée avec la bière, étaler le fromage et mettre au four.

Soupe à l'oignon

Ingrédients

Faire fondre les oignons émincés en rondelles et l'ail haché dans le beurre. Ajouter le Tabasco, le poivre, la muscade et le bouillon de viande. Mélanger et laisser cuire, à couvert et à feu doux pendant 20 minutes. Préchauffer le four à 230°C (th. 8). Faire griller les tranches de pain. Hors du feu, incorporer le vin blanc à la soupe. Verser la soupe dans 4 soupières individuelles. Étaler le fromage râpé sur les tranches de pain placées sur la soupe. Faire gratiner au four.

600 g d'oignons
1 gousse d'ail
100 g de beurre
1,25 litre de bouillon de viande
25 cl de vin blanc sec
4 tranches de pain blanc
50 g d'emmenthal râpé
1 demi-cuillère à café de Tabasco
1 pointe de noix de muscade râpée
1 pointe de poivre de Cayenne

RECETTES

Salade Deux Magots

Ingrédients

Laver et essorer la salade, puis découper les feuilles en morceaux égaux. Couper les tomates en quartiers, le jambon en lamelles, les œufs durs en quatre, le poulet et le comté en dés. Disposer le tout dans un saladier. Assaisonner avec une vinaigrette composée selon votre goût et servir immédiatement.

Belle laitue (ou salade de saison)

3 tranches de jambon de Paris

2 blancs de poulet cuit

300 g de comté

4 tomates

4 œufs durs

Huile d'olive

Ciboulette

Vinaigre balsamique

Sel, poivre

Salade parisienne

Effiler et laver les haricots. Porter à ébullition 25 cl d'eau salée et faire cuire les haricots pendant 15 minutes. Égoutter. Peler et hacher l'échalotte. Mettre les haricots et les cerneaux de noix dans un saladier. Mélanger l'échalote, le vinaigre, 1 pincée de sel et verser l'huile sans cesser de battre. Verser la sauce sur la salade et mélanger délicatement. Laisser reposer la salade à température ambiante pendant 2 heures. Couper le foie gras en fines tranches et garnir la salade.

Ingrédients

150 g de foie gras (ou magret de canard)

50 g de cerneaux de noix

500 g de haricots verts

1 échalote

4 cuillerées à soupe d'huile de noix

3 cuillerées à soupe de vinaigre de Xérès

Salade niçoise

Laver, essorer et tailler la salade. Laver les tomates et les couper en rondelles ou en tranches. Laver et couper le poivron. Peler et émincer l'oignon. Émietter le thon. Couper les œufs en rondelles ou en tranches. Mélanger l'huile, le vinaigre, du sel, du poivre et verser cette sauce sur la salade.

Ingrédients

200 g de thon à l'huile

12 olives noires

2 œufs durs

1 laitue

500 g de tomates

1 poivron rouge ou vert

1 oignon

3 cuillerées à soupe d'huile d'olive

1 cuillerée à soupe et demie de vinaigre

Steak tartare

Hacher la viande à la grosse grille ou au couteau.
Préparer l'assaisonnement dans un récipient.
Mettre le jaune d'œuf et une cuillère à café de
moutarde, du sel et du poivre.
Monter le tout comme une mayonnaise avec l'huile.
Rajouter la sauce anglaise, le ketchup,
une pointe de Tabasco.
Bien mélanger l'ensemble.
Incorporer ensuite le persil haché, l'oignon haché et les
câpres à quantité égale.
Une fois les condiments bien mélangés,
mettre la viande hachée,
puis malaxer le tout.

Ingrédients

180 g d'aiguillette Baronne
1 jaune d'œuf
Persil haché
Oignon haché
Câpres
Huile
Moutarde
Tabasco
Sauce anglaise
Ketchup

Œufs coque

Ingrédients

Œufs très frais
Tranches de pain
Beurre demi-sel
Sel fin

Plonger les œufs délicatement
dans de l'eau bouillante salée.
Laisser cuire pendant
3 minutes à partir de la
reprise de l'ébullition.
Servir aussitôt dans des
coquetiers avec des mouillettes
de pain beurré.

Œufs en gelée

Faire ramollir la gélatine dans de l'eau froide, puis la faire fondre dans le bouillon chaud avec l'estragon et le cerfeuil. Faire bouillir 2 litres d'eau avec du vinaigre. Casser délicatement chaque œuf dans un bol et les faire glisser dans l'eau frémissante. Les laisser pocher pendant 3 minutes. Les retirer avec une écumoire et les mettre dans de l'eau froide.
Tapisser le fond des ramequins d'une fine couche de gelée. Déposer des lamelles de jambon et 1 feuille d'estragon. Napper de gelée et placer les œufs pochés. Décorer avec des lamelles de truffes et de l'estragon. Couvrir de gelée. Placer au réfrigérateur pendant 3 heures.

Ingrédients

4 œufs
1 tomate
Quelques lamelles de jambon blanc
4 lamelles de truffe
10 cl de vinaigre de vin blanc
50 cl de bouillon de volaille
6 feuilles de gélatine
Quelques feuilles d'estragon
Cerfeuil haché

Omelette mixte jambon et fromage

Avec une fourchette battre les œufs et la crème dans un saladier. Ajouter le jambon haché en fines lamelles, le fromage, le sel, le poivre et les fines herbes. Faire chauffer une cuillère d'huile et une noisette de beurre dans une poêle. Verser le contenu du saladier dans la poêle en le répartissant délicatement avec une spatule en bois. Laisser cuire selon votre goût.

Ingrédients

6 œufs
3 tranches de jambon de Paris
200 g de gruyère râpé
2 cuillères à soupe de crème fraîche
Fines herbes : estragon, ciboulette
Huile, beurre
Sel, poivre

Tarte aux pommes

Ingrédients

6 belles pommes
250 g de farine
125 g de beurre
1 cuillère à café d'huile
1 demi verre d'eau
120 g de sucre en poudre

Préparer la pâte en mélangeant la farine, le beurre,
l'huile et le verre d'eau.
Former une boule et laisser reposer.
Dans une casserole verser les 200 g de sucre avec de l'eau
et mélanger jusqu'à obtention d'un caramel onctueux.
Précuire les pommes coupées en quartiers dans une casserole avec
un peu de beurre. Répartir la pâte dans un moule à tarte
en faisant des trous avec une fourchette, verser
le caramel et placer les pommes. Enfourner (th.8) pendant
45 minutes. Laisser refroidir, puis démouler.

Opéra

Ingrédients

Biscuit :

70 g de jaunes d'œufs

115 g de blanc d'œufs

120 g de sucre

25 de pâte d'amande

215 g de poudre d'amande brune

Ganache :

400 g de chocolat

350 g de crème liquide

Crème au beurre :

3 œufs + 1 jaune

380 g de sucre

15 cl d'eau

380 g de beurre

20 g de café soluble

Glaçage :

80 g de couverture fondante

80 g de crème

Fouetter les jaunes d'œufs avec 30 g de sucre et la pâte d'amande. Ajouter les amandes en poudre. Monter les blancs avec le sucre restant et les incorporer délicatement. Cuire ce biscuit à 220° C (th. 7-8) pendant 8 à 10 minutes.

Faire fondre le chocolat et le mélanger à la crème. Réserver en fouettant de temps en temps.

Porter le sucre et l'eau à ébullition. Verser sur les œufs. Monter au fouet jusqu'à refroidissement. Ajouter le beurre et continuer à fouetter. Incorporer le café dissous dans un peu d'eau.

Diviser le biscuit en trois parties égales. Sur l'une des parties, étendre la ganache. Étaler la crème au beurre-café sur la deuxième partie. Recouvrir de la dernière partie et réserver au frais.

Faire bouillir la crème et la verser sur le chocolat. Mélanger et glacer le dessus.

Chocolat chaud

Ingrédients

Pour 1 litre de lait :

250 ml de crème fleurette

350 g de chocolat en pistole

(de chez Barry/Callebaut)

1 trait de vanille

Porter le lait à ébullition avec la vanille, incorporer le chocolat, ajouter la crème, faire bouillir 1 minute.

INDEX DES NOMS CITÉS

Index

BIBLIOGRAPHIE

Audouin Philippe, *Les Surréalistes*, Seuil, Paris, 1973
Buisson Sylvie, Parisot Christian, *Paris-Montmartre, les artistes et les lieux 1860-1920*, Terrail, Paris, 1996
Caracalla Jean-Paul, *Montparnasse, l'âge d'or*, Denoël, Paris, 1997
Caracalla Jean-Paul, *Saint-Germain-des-Prés*, Flammarion, Paris, 1993
Cau Jean, *Une nuit à Saint-Germain-des-Prés*, Robert Laffont, Paris, 1977
Cazes Marcellin, *50 ans de Lipp*, La Jeune Parque, Paris, 1966
Clert Iris, *Iris time ou l'artventure*, Denoël, 1978
Crespelle Jean-Pierre, *La Vie quotidienne à Montparnasse*, Hachette, Paris, 19676
Crespelle Jean-Pierre, *Montparnasse vivant*, Hachette, Paris, 1962
Donnay Maurice, *Autour du Chat Noir*, Grasset, Paris, 1942
Drot Jean-Marie, *Les Heures chaudes de Montparnasse*, Hazan, Paris, 1995
Durand-Boubal Christophe, *Café de Flore, mémoire d'un siècle*, Indigo, Paris, 1992
Farguier Léon, *Saint-Germain-des-Prés mon village*, Plon, Paris, 1938
Hanoteau Guillaume, *L'Âge d'or de Saint-Germain-des-Prés*, Denoël, Paris, 1965
Hofmarcher Arnaud, *Les Deux Magots, chronique d'un café littéraire*, Le Cherche-Midi éditeur, Paris, 1994
Klüver Billy, *Un jour avec Picasso*, Hazan, Paris, 1994
Labracherie Pierre, *La Vie quotidienne de la bohème littéraire au XIX' siècle*, Hachette, Paris, 1967
Lemaire Gérard-Georges, *L'Europe des cafés*, Eric Koehler, Paris, 1991
Lemaire Gérard-Georges, *Théories des cafés*, IMEC/Eric Koehler, Paris, 1997
Lemaire Gérard-Georges, *Les Cafés littéraires*, éditions de La Différence, Paris, 1997
La Vie quotidienne à Montmartre au temps de Picasso, Hachette, Paris, 1978
Le Roman de Pascin, André Bay, Albin Michel, 1984
Les Années Montparnasse, Contrejour/Le Monde, Paris, 1990
Mac Orlan Pierre, *Montmartre, souvenirs*, Les éditions de Chabassol, Bruxelles, 1926
Nadeau Maurice, *Histoire du surréalisme*, Seuil, Paris, 1964
Olivier Fernande, *Picasso et ses amis*, Stock, Paris, 1933
Philippon Henri, *Almanach de Saint-Germain-des-Prés*, L'Ermite, Paris, 1950
Planiol François, *La Coupole*, Denoël, Paris, 1986
Rude Maxime, *Tout-Paris au café*, Maurice Dreyfous éditeur, Paris, 1877
Salmon André, André Bonne, *Montparnasse*, Paris, 1950
Salmon André, *Souvenirs sans fin*, Gallimard, 1961
Warnod André, *Bals, cafés et cabarets*, Eugène Figuière & Co éditeur, Paris, 1913

Littérature
Alexandre Maxime, *Mémoires d'un surréaliste*, La Jeune Parque, Paris, 1968
Apollinaire Guillaume, *Le Flâneur des deux rives*, Gallimard, Paris, 1928
Aragon Louis, *Le Paysan de Paris*, Gallimard, Paris, 1926
Balzac Honoré de, *À Paris*, éditions Complexe, Bruxelles, 1993
Beauvoir Simone de, *Mémoires d'une jeune fille rangée*, Gallimard, Paris, 1958
Beauvoir Simone de, *La Force des choses*, Gallimard, Paris, 1977
Billy André, *La Terrasse du Luxembourg*, Librairie Arthème Fayard, Paris, 1945
Billy André, *L'Époque contemporaine*, Tallandier, Paris, 1956
Carco Francis, *L'Ami des peintres*, éditions du Milieu du Monde, Genève, 1944
Carco Francis, *Mémoires d'une autre vie*, éditions du Milieu du Monde, Genève, 1944
Carco Francis, *Nostalgie de Paris*, éditions du Milieu du Monde, Genève, 1941
Cazalis Anne-Marie, *Les Mémoires d'une Anne*, Stock, Paris, 1976
Dorgelès Roland, *Au beau temps de la butte*, Albin Michel, Paris, 1943
Dorgelès Roland, *Bouquet de Bohème*, Albin Michel, Paris, 1947
Fargue Léon-Paul, *Le Piéton de Paris*, Gallimard, Paris, 1932
Fels Florent, *Le Roman de l'art vivant*, Arthème Fayard, Paris, 1959
Flanner Janet, *Paris, c'était hier*, Mazarine, Paris, 1981
Frank Nino, *Le Bruit parmi le vent*, Paris, 1968
Georges-Michel Michel, *Les Montparnos*, Arthème Fayard, Paris, 1923
Gide André, *Les Faux-Monnayeurs*, Gallimard, Paris, 1925-1926
Goncourt Edmond et Jules de, *Journal, Mémoires de la vie littéraire*, Bouquins, Robert Laffont, Paris, 1989
Gréco Juliette, *Jujube*, Stock, Paris, 1982
Hemingway Ernest, *Paris est une fête*, Gallimard, Paris, 1964
Leduc Violette, *La Folie en tête*, Gallimard, Paris, 1970
Monnier Adrienne, *Rue de l'Odéon*, Albin Michel, Paris, 1960
Moore Georges, *Confessions d'un jeune Anglais*, Christian Bourgois éditeur, Paris, 1986
Vian Boris, *Manuel de Saint-Germain-des-Prés*, Le Chêne, Paris, 1974

CRÉDITS PHOTOGRAPHIQUES

couverture Martin Schreiber
Pages 6/7 : Léonard de Selva
8 : Léonard de Selva
9 : Montmartre des Arts, Paris
10 : D.R. ; Montmartre des Arts
11 : Archive Photos ; Léonard de Selva
12 : Archive Photos ; Giraudon ;
   Giraudon
13 : Giraudon
14 : Montmartre des Arts ; Giraudon
15 : Giraudon ; Montmartre des Arts
16 : Archive Photos ; D.R.
17 : D.R.
18 : Archive Photos ; D.R ; D.R ; D.R.
19 : Montmartre des Arts ;
   Archive Photos ; IMEC.
20 : Giraudon
21 : Archive Photos
22 : D.R.
23 : D.R. ; Montmartre des Arts
24 : Archive Photos ;
   Montmartre des Arts
25 : Léonard de Selva
26 : Archive Photos ; Léonard de Selva
27 : Archive Photos
28 : D.R. ; Montmartre des Arts
29 : Montmartre des Arts ;
   Archive Photos
30 : Archive Photos ; D.R.
31 : D.R. ; Archive Photos
34 : Xavier Richer
35 : Xavier Richer ; Tao
36 : Tao
37 : Tao
38 : Xavier Richer

39 : Xavier Richer
40 : Tao
41 : Xavier Richer
42/43 : Léonard de Selva
44 : Léonard de Selva
45 : D.R.
46 : Léonard de Selva
47 : Giraudon ; Archives Artistiques
48/49 : Roger-Viollet
50 : Roger-Viollet
51 : Archive Photos
52 : Archive Photos ;
   Roger-Viollet
53 : Archive Photos
54 : Archive Photos ;
   Montmartre des Arts
55 : Archives légales A. Modigliani,
   Paris ; Archive Photos
56/57 : Archive Photos
58 : Archive Photos ; IMEC.
59 : Giraudon ; Keystone
60 : IMEC.
61 : Archive Photos
62 : Archive Photos
63 : Archive Photos
64 : D.R.
65 : Archive Photos
66 : Archive Photos
67 : Archive Photos
68/69 : Keystone
70 : IMEC.
71 : Archives Pascin, Paris ; D.R.
72 : IMEC.
73 : IMEC. ;
   Archives artistiques, Sylvie Buisson

76-93 : Martin Schreiber
94/95 : © Pierre Jahan, collection
Deux Magots
96 : Léonard de Selva
97 : Léonard de Selva
98 : Giraudon
99 : D.R. ; IMEC.
100 : D.R.
101 : IMEC. ; Procope
102 : Roger-Viollet
103 : Roger-Viollet
104 : Edimédia
105 : D.R. ; © Willy Ronis/Rapho
106 : © Charbonnier ; D.R.
107 : Archive Photos
108/109 : © Fonds France-Soir
110 : D.R
111 : J.-P. Caracalla ; © Ostier
112 : © Seeberger
113 : Explorer ; D.R.
114 : Roger-Viollet
115 : J.P. Caracalla ; D.R.
116 : Roger-Viollet ;
   Collection Deux Magots
117 : © Robert Doisneau / Rapho
118 : Archive Photos
119 : Léonard de Selva ;
   Archive Photos ;
   Edimédia
120 : D.R. ; Roger-Viollet
121 : Roger-Viollet ;
   Brasserie Lipp
122 : Collection Lipp
123 : Archive Photos
126-171 : Martin Schreiber

Achevé d'imprimer sur les presses
d'Amilcare Pizzi, Italie.

Aux Closerie des Lilas
d'un client fidèle 1920 - 1956
Ernest Hemingway

Henry Miller — "th[e]
who passed man[y]
day here — s[o]

Mon remerciement pour
l'aimable accueil Et
à bientôt Eugène Ionesco

Une bonne Maison
de Gaîté.
Guy de [...]

Quel l'honneur d'être à la
Closerie des Lilas. Je fais la bise à tous!
Robert Sabatier

S. de Be[auvoir]

Combien prête-t-on, au Mont-de-Piété, sur
les livres d'or?
A. Breffort

Quand il est mort le poète
Quand il est mort le poète
Tous ses amis
Tous ses amis
Tous ses amis pleuraient
quand il est mort le poète
quand il est mort le poète
le monde entier
le monde entier
le monde entier pleurait ...
. . . .
Louis Amade
13 - X . 66

Une cette seule écriture suffise.
d'un client presque aussi fidèle
qu'Hemingway
Jean-Louis ...

très heureux
à la closerie
ma vingtième a[nnée]
[...]

A l'occasion des Deux
Sal[...]

Walking Eye
mobile app

Discover the world's best destinations with the Insight Guides Walking Eye app, available to download for free in the App Store and Google Play.

The container app provides easy access to fantastic free content on events and activities taking place in your current location or chosen destination, with the possibility of booking, as well as the regularly-updated Insight Guides travel blog: Inspire Me. In addition, you can purchase curated, premium destination guides through the app, which feature local highlights, hotel, bar, restaurant and shopping listings, an A to Z of practical information and more. Or purchase and download Insight Guides eBooks straight to your device.

TOP 10 ATTRACTIONS

EDINBURGH
The capital has everything: a castle, a palace, a parliament, an international arts festival, haute cuisine... See page 27.

CULZEAN CASTLE
Spectacularly positioned on a cliff's edge, it dates from the 16th century. See page 46.

GLEN COE
Its stunning scenery is a magnet for hikers. See page 74.

BURRELL COLLECTION
Glasgow's treasure trove of outstanding art. See page 51.

LOCH LOMOND
Britain's largest freshwater lake has fired the imagination of many a composer and writer, including Sir Walter Scott. See page 57.

SKYE
The atmospheric isle has a number of dramatic rock formations. See page 81.

BURNS COUNTRY
The Burns Heritage Trail runs from Alloway to Dumfries. See page 44.

URQUHART CASTLE
A romantic ruin by Loch Ness that may have been the site of a Pictish fort. See page 71.

INVEREWE GARDEN
Overlooking Loch Ewe, here subtropical flora and fauna thrive. See page 75.

ST ANDREWS
On the Fife coast is the home of golf and Scotland's oldest university. See page 59.

A PERFECT DAY

9.00am

Breakfast

The ideal place to start a day of culture is at the Scottish Café inside the Scottish National Gallery, on Princes Street. Set yourself up with a traditional breakfast before a look around the gallery.

12.30pm

Shopping

Off George V Bridge, visit Victoria Street with its specialist shops, and continue on into the Grassmarket for lots of lunch options. Retrace your steps and continue to High Street, where St Giles Cathedral dominates.

2.00pm

Royal Mile

Continue down the Royal Mile, where you will find notable attractions including the Museum of Childhood, John Knox House, the Museum of Edinburgh and Canongate Tolbooth. Near the end of the road, the Scottish Parliament Building looms into view and at the foot of the Royal Mile stands the Palace of Holyroodhouse.

10.00am

Edinburgh Castle

Follow the Mound, crossing Princes Street Gardens towards the Old Town and climb the steep steps up to the castle. It's worth getting to the castle early to avoid the crowds. From here there are great views across the New Town below.

11.30am

Castle Hill

Walk back down Castle Hill, passing attractions such as the Scotch Whisky Experience, Camera Obscura and Gladstone's Land, along the way. Take time to explore the vennels and wynds as you go.

4.00pm

Afternoon tea
Walk back up the Royal Mile. Just past the Scottish Parliament building is Clarinda's Tearoom, a great pit stop to indulge in tea and home-baked treats.

7.30pm

Dinner
After freshening up at your hotel, head to the New Town – in and around George Street, good places to eat are endless. If Italian cooking is your preference, try the ever-popular Gusto or Contini. For a special occasion, Number One boasts a Michelin star.

3.00pm

Holyroodhouse
It is worth taking time to see the fine collection of royal artefacts (if the royal family are not in residence); alternatively, if weather allows, explore the huge expanse of Holyrood Park behind.

9.30pm

On the town
You couldn't be in a better spot to finish the night in a chic bar or nightclub. On George Street, pop into the Opal Lounge for cocktails and then move onto Lulu, a trendy club located beneath the Tigerlilly hotel; or perhaps sip a Foxtrot Fizz or Red Rum at Bramble in nearby Queen Street.

CONTENTS

INTRODUCTION

Scotland is a land steeped in romantic tradition. Its distinctive dress, its national drink, its famous bagpipe music and its stormy history give it an image recognisable worldwide. Though Scotland's territory is small, it has an unrivalled variety of landscape: deep green glens that slice through rugged mountains; forbidding castles reflected in dark, peat-stained lochs; moors awash with purple heather or yellow broom and gorse; green fields and hills dotted with sheep; and a wildly irregular coastline, incessantly pounded by the Atlantic and the North Sea, with both forbidding cliffs and sweeping sandy beaches.

Scotland's Highlands and Islands are a riot of spectacular natural beauty and one of the few remaining wilderness frontiers in all of Europe. Within easy reach of the cities of Edinburgh, Glasgow and Aberdeen are vast tracts of unspoiled country. You might see red deer break cover and golden eagles, or even an osprey, swooping overhead. In coursing streams, magnificent salmon and trout challenge the angler, while seals lounge on rocky shores. It's quite possible to walk all day and not see another human being.

The sea flows in to fill many of the country's 300 lochs (except for the Lake of Menteith, Scots never call them 'lakes'); others are fresh water. The rolling hills and tranquil rivers of the south and the rich farmland of Fife and Royal Deeside present gentler but no less enticing landscapes.

The cultural mosaic, like the scenery, is hugely varied. Every summer Edinburgh, the intellectually and architecturally stimulating capital, is the scene of a distinguished international festival of music and the arts; and Glasgow is a former 'European City of Culture'. Both cities have outstanding museums and the Burrell Collection in Glasgow is one of Europe's great art galleries. All around the country you'll find theatre festivals, concerts, Highland gatherings, folk shows and crafts exhibitions.

You can visit some 150 castles – some intact, others respectable ruins. There are also baronial mansions, ancient abbeys and archeological sites that invite exploration.

GEOGRAPHY AND CLIMATE

Covering the northernmost third of the United Kingdom, Scotland's 77,700 sq miles (30,000 sq km) are home to more than 5 million people, making up one-tenth of the total population of Great Britain. Scotland's territorial area includes 790 islands, of which 130 are inhabited. Some are popular tourist destinations easily reached by ferry or plane.

Happily, what people say about Scotland's weather isn't always true. Between May and October there are hours and even whole days of hot sunshine interrupting the rain, mist and bracing winds which perhaps keep the Scots so hardy. Sightseers and photographers appreciate the amazing visibility to be had on clear days. Around lochs and on the coast the only drawback is the midge. These pesky biting flies are impossible to avoid at the beginning and end of the day during the summer. The cold, snowy winters have made the Highlands Britain's skiing centre, for both downhill and cross-country skiing, with Glen Coe having the steepest runs.

Stags in the Scottish Highlands

POLITICS AND IDENTITY

Glen Coe

Constitutionally linked to England for nearly three centuries, Scotland is a land that keeps proudly unto itself. It prints its own bank notes and maintains independent educational and judicial systems, its own church and its own Parliament. Gaelic is still spoken in the Western Highlands and Islands. This independent spirit has strengthened with the growth of the Scottish National Party who instigated the 2014 referendum and crushed the other parties in Scotland in the 2015 general election. Despite this surge in nationalism, the country is divided on whether to leave the United Kingdom and many of its citizens wish to remain in the union.

You'll meet with a friendly welcome everywhere. Smiles are genuine, humour is jovially sharp. Hospitality is an ancient tradition and nowhere will you find people who are more courteous, or more willing to go out of their way for you. Scots have a reputation for tight-fistedness but generosity among friends and strangers is much more common. Scots have a great respect for education – by the 17th century Scotland had four universities while England still had only two.

Scotland is famous for golf, but the one subject that's certain to fire the hearts of most Scots is football, with the rivalry between two Glasgow teams, Rangers and Celtic, inspiring passionate debate. The national team also arouses fierce loyalties.

Religious observance is still a factor in the Highlands and Islands, but elsewhere the former blue laws that once kept everything closed down on Sunday are giving way.

TRUE GRIT

Over the centuries the hard-working Scots have made their mark on all corners of the globe: they were frontiersmen in North America, explorers in Africa, pioneers in Australia. Intellectually, the contribution made by Scots to world science, medicine and industry has been little short of astonishing. Above all, what binds the Scots together is a love of country plus a strong sense of community and national identity.

All over Scotland you will see and hear the exhortation to 'Haste ye back' ('Come back soon'). After sampling the extraordinary beauty and diversity of this delightful country, you'll want to do just that.

KILTS AND TARTANS

Brightly coloured tartan kilts have been worn in the Highlands since the Middle Ages but most of the tartans we see today date from the early 19th century when the British royal family made the Highlands fashionable. Daytime Highland dress consists of a knee-length kilt, matching waistcoat and tweed jacket, long knitted socks (with a sgian dubh stuck in the right stocking), and flashes. A sporran (purse) hangs from the waist, and a plaid (sort of tartan rug) is sometimes flung over the shoulder.

The Clearances in the aftermath of the Battle of Culloden in 1746 destroyed the clan system and Highland dress was forbidden. The kilt survived only because the Highland regiments, recruited to help defeat Napoleon, were allowed to continue to wear it. Authentic tartans are registered designs, and each clan has its own pattern. As the clans subdivided, many variations (setts) were produced. Today, there are some 2,500 designs in all. To find out more, visit the Edinburgh Old Town Weaving Company at 555 Castlehill, Edinburgh (open daily).

A BRIEF HISTORY

Scotland's earliest settlers are thought to have been Celtic-Iberians who worked their way up from the Mediterranean – they have left us evidence of their presence in the cairns and standing stones which are found all over the country. In recent years, archaeologists discovered the remains of a huge timbered building west of Aberdeen which pre-dates Stonehenge by 1,000 years.

By the time the Romans invaded Scotland in AD 84, the inhabitants of the northern region were the Picts, whom they dubbed 'the painted people'. The Roman legions defeated the Picts but were spread too thin to hold 'Caledonia', as they called the area. They withdrew behind the line of Hadrian's Wall, close to and south of the present Scottish-English border. The Picts left little evidence of their culture or language.

CHRISTIANITY AND THE NORSE INVASION

A Gaelic-speaking tribe from Ireland, the Scots founded a shaky kingdom in Argyll known as 'Dalriada'. In the late 4th century a Scot, St Ninian, travelled to Rome and, on his return, introduced Christianity to Dalriada. His colleague, St Mungo, established the foundation that is now the Cathedral of Glasgow. However, Christianity remained fairly isolated until the arrival in 563 of the great missionary from Ireland, St Columba. For more than 30 years, from the remote island of Iona, he spread the faith that would eventually provide the basis for the unification of Scotland. Tiny Iona today remains one of the most venerated sites in Christendom.

In the late 8th century the Vikings swarmed over Europe setting up strongholds in the Orkneys and Hebrides and on the northern mainland. The Norsemen were to hold the Western Islands, Orkney and the Shetlands for hundreds of years.

UNIFICATION AND FEUDALISM IN THE SOUTH

The unifying influence of Christianity allowed an early chieftain, Kenneth MacAlpin, to unite the Scots and the Picts in 843. In 1018 this kingdom, led by Malcolm II, defeated the Northumbrians from the south at the Battle of Carham and extended its domain to the present southern boundary of Scotland. The 'murder most foul' of Malcolm's grandson, Duncan II, by Macbeth of Moray was the inspiration for Shakespeare's Scottish tragedy.

Malcolm III, also known as Malcolm Canmore, changed the course of Scottish history when he married an English princess in 1069. This was the highly pious Queen Margaret who was later canonised. She brought a powerful English influence to the Scottish scene and sought to implement a radical change, replacing the Gaelic-speaking culture of Scotland and its Celtic church with the English-speaking culture and institutions of the south and the church of Rome.

The rift that Margaret created was widened by her son, David I (reigned 1124–53). He embarked on a huge building programme, founding the great abbeys of Melrose and Jedburgh. He also brought Norman influence into Scotland and introduced to the Lowlands a French-speaking aristocracy and a

St Margaret's Chapel, Edinburgh

feudal system of land ownership based on the Anglo-Norman model. He was not successful, however, in imposing this system on the north, where the social structure was based on kinship and where the clan chieftain held land, not for himself, but for his people.

THE SHAPING OF SCOTLAND

The death of King Alexander III (1249–86) in a riding accident touched off a succession crisis that began what was to be the long, bloody struggle for Scottish independence. The English king, Edward I, was invited to arbitrate among the claimants to the throne. He seized his opportunity and installed John Balliol as his vassal king of Scots. But in 1295 Balliol renounced his fealty to Edward and allied himself with France. In retaliation the English king sacked the burgh of Berwick, crushed the Scots at Dunbar, swept north, seized the great castles and took from Scone Palace the Sacred Stone of Destiny on which

WILLIAM WALLACE

After a comparatively peaceful interlude, England's insidious interference provoked a serious backlash in 1297. William Wallace, a violent youth from Elderslie, became an outlaw after a scuffle with English soldiers in which a girl (some think she was his wife) who helped him escape was killed herself by the Sheriff of Lanark. Wallace returned to kill the sheriff, but didn't stop there; soon he had raised enough of an army to drive back the English, making him for some months master of southern Scotland. But Wallace wasn't supported by the nobles, who considered him low-born and, after being defeated at Falkirk by England's Edward I, he was hanged, drawn and quartered. His quarters were sent to Newcastle, Berwick, Stirling and Perth.

William Wallace rallies his Scottish forces against the English

all Scottish monarchs had been crowned. Edward had earned his title 'Hammer of the Scots'. Scotland seemed crushed. However, one man, William Wallace, rose up and led a revolt, soundly defeating the English at Stirling Bridge. Edward responded by routing Wallace at Falkirk. In 1305, Wallace was captured, taken to London and brutally executed.

Robert the Bruce then took up the cause. After he was crowned king at Scone in 1306, he was forced to flee to Ireland. The story goes that when he was most discouraged, he watched a spider spinning a web and, inspired by this example of perseverance and courage, he resolved never to give up hope. The next year he returned to Scotland and captured Perth and Edinburgh. In 1314 at Bannockburn, he faced an army that outnumbered his forces three to one and had superior weapons. However, Bruce had chosen his ground and his strategy skilfully and won a decisive victory. Bruce continued to hammer away at the English until 1328, when Edward III signed a treaty recognising the independence of

Scotland. Robert the Bruce died the following year, honoured as Scotland's saviour.

THE STEWARTS

In 1371 the reign of the Stewart, or Stuart, dynasty began. While the family was intelligent and talented, it seemed also prone to tragedy. The first three kings all came to power while still children; James I, II and II all died relatively young in tragic circumstances. James IV, who ruled 1488–1513, was an able king who quashed the rebellious Macdonald clan chiefs who had been styling themselves 'Lords of the Isles' since the mid-14th century. In 1513 there was disaster: to honour the 'auld alliance' with France, James led his Scottish troops in an invasion over the English border. In the Battle of Flodden that followed, the Scots were crushed by the English in their worst ever defeat. About 10,000 lost their lives, including the king himself and most of the peerage. One result of the battle was to bring infant James V to the throne. His French second wife, Mary of Guise-Lorraine was the mother of Mary, Queen of Scots. James died prematurely in 1542, six days after his wife had given birth to his heir.

The Apprentice Pillar in the 15th-century Rosslyn Chapel

MARY, QUEEN OF SCOTS

The tragic events of this queen's life have captivated the imagination of generations. After the infant Mary was crowned, Henry VIII tried to force the betrothal of Mary to his son, Edward and thus unite the two crowns. At the age of five Mary was sent to France for safekeeping. Her pro-Catholic mother, supported by French forces, took over as regent, a move that was not popular with most Scots.

> ### Flodden Wall
>
> Following the Battle of Flodden, the residents of Edinburgh hastily built the Flodden Wall to protect the city from sacking. A section of the wall still survives in the Vennel (alley) just off the Grassmarket.

At the age of 15, Mary was married to the heir to the French throne. He died soon after becoming king, however, and in 1561 Mary, a devout young Catholic widow, returned to Scotland to assume her throne. There she found the Protestant Reformation in full swing, led by John Knox. A follower of Geneva Protestant John Calvin, Knox was a bitter enemy of both the Roman Catholic and the Anglican Church. Mary's agenda was bound to cause trouble: to restore Roman Catholicism and to rule as queen of Scotland in the French style. The Scottish monarchs had been kings of the Scots, not of Scotland so they were answerable to the people – a fundamental difference. She alienated the lords who held the real power and came into conflict with Knox, who heaped insults on her in public.

Mary spent just six turbulent years as Scotland's queen. Scandals surrounded her. In 1565 she married Henry, Lord Darnley and the next year bore a son, the future James VI. Darnley was implicated in the murder of Mary's confidential secretary at Holyroodhouse. Darnley himself was murdered two years later and many suspected Mary's involvement.

Mary, Queen of Scots

Doubts crystallised when, a few months later, she married one of the plot's ringleaders, the Earl of Bothwell. Deposed and held captive, she made a daring escape to England, there to become a thorn in the side of her cousin, Elizabeth I and a rallying point for Catholic dissidents. Mary was kept in captivity in England for nearly 20 years until, in 1587, she was finally beheaded.

TOWARDS UNION WITH ENGLAND

After his mother's death, James VI assumed the throne as Scotland's first Protestant king. When Elizabeth died in 1603, James rode south to claim the English throne as James I. But the Union of Crowns did not bring instant harmony. The 17th century witnessed fierce religious and political struggles in Scotland. James and his son Charles I (1625–49) had to face opposition from Scottish churchmen. In 1638 Scots signed the National Covenant, giving them the right to their own form of Presbyterian worship.

When the civil war broke out in England, the Covenanters at first backed Parliament against Charles. After he was beheaded in 1649, the Scots backed Charles II. However, Presbyterianism was not formally established as the Church of Scotland until Catholic James VII (James II of England) was deposed in the Glorious Revolution of 1688, which brought Protestant joint monarchs, William III and Mary II of Orange to the English throne (1689–1702). In 1707, despite widespread

Scottish opposition, England and Scotland signed the Act of Union. The Scots were to have minority representation in the upper and lower houses at Westminster, they were to keep their own courts and legal system and the status of the national Presbyterian Church was guaranteed. But Scottish nationalism was not so easily subdued.

THE JACOBITES

Four times in the next 40 years the Jacobites tried to restore the exiled royal family to the throne. The most serious effort was the Rising Stewart, known as 'Bonnie Prince Charlie'. This grandson of James VII was 24 years old when he sailed from France disguised as a divinity student to land in Scotland in July 1745. Within two months he had rallied enough clan support to occupy Perth and Edinburgh. In early November he invaded England, pushing to Derby by 4 December.

However, English Jacobites failed to come to the aid of the rebellion and again, no help appeared from France. Charles' troops were hopelessly outnumbered. Reluctantly he agreed to retreat north and, by 20 December, they were back in Scotland. From this time on, the Jacobite cause went downhill. The final blow

Bonnie Prince Charlie

came at the Battle of Culloden Moor which was fought near Inverness on 16 April 1746. The weary Highlanders were subjected to a crushing defeat at the hands of superior government forces under the Duke of Cumberland. In less than an hour, about 1,200 of Charles's men were killed; many others, wounded and captured, were treated in a brutal manner that earned Cumberland the lasting sobriquet of 'Butcher'. Charles escaped, aided by Flora MacDonald, who became Scotland's romantic heroine. After spending five months as a fugitive in the Highlands and Western Isles, he left his country for good aboard a French ship.

THE AFTERMATH

Although the Jacobite cause was finished, Highlanders had to face harsh consequences. The clan structure was destroyed, Gaelic suppressed and wearing of the kilt or plaid was banned. Clans who had supported the rebellion lost their lands. Thousands of crofters (farmers of smallholdings) had to abandon their homes to wealthy sheep farmers from the south under the Highland Clearances programme. Many emigrated to the United States and Canada. Today the Highland glens still remain empty.

While the Highlands were emptying, the less troubled part of Scotland was booming. Glasgow's tobacco monopoly enriched its merchants and James Watt's invention of the steam engine made the Industrial Revolution possible. Glasgow,

Stewart standard

Bonnie Prince Charlie arrived at Glenfinnan on 19 August 1745 and raised the Stewart standard. He rallied 1,200 clansmen ready to battle for the British throne. Seventy years later, Alexander MacDonald of Glenaladale built the Glenfinnan Memorial in memory of all the clansmen who had fought for the cause.

Bonnie Prince Charlie raised the Stewart standard at Glenfinnan

with its famous shipbuilding industry, became the 'Workshop of the Empire'. Edinburgh began development into an international intellectual and cultural centre. The so-called 'Scottish Enlightenment' produced philosophers like David Hume and poets like Robert Burns.

Unlike England, with its rigid class system, Scotland's more democratic attitude made it far easier for poor boys to gain a university education. The work of Scottish scientists, writers, explorers, engineers and industrialists became famous worldwide. In the 1860s Queen Victoria and Prince Albert discovered the Highlands and made tartan apparel fashionable by adopting it themselves.

Yet with the political centre in Westminster and a system in place that gave precedence to English affairs, Scotland was never an equal partner in the union with England. During the privations of the Great Depression and the industrial downturn after World War II, Scots felt impotent and apathetic. But when North Sea oil was discovered, the failing Scottish

Scottish Parliament building

economy did a turnaround, and with the new prosperity came a resurgence of Scottish national spirit.

MODERN SCOTLAND

In 1997 the Scots voted overwhelmingly for the re-establishment of a Scottish Parliament. The new Scottish Parliament, which opened in 1999, gained control over all local affairs, such as education, economic development, agriculture and the environment, but with a limited ability to collect and control tax revenues. Nonetheless, many Scots saw this as a new beginning, a chance to assert their national identity and protect their culture and heritage. A state-of-the-art new Scottish Parliament building – way over budget and well past its original completion deadline – opened for business at Holyrood in 2004.

In the 2007 Scottish election, the Scottish National Party gained power by a one-seat majority with its leader, Alex Salmond, firmly installed as First Minister of the country. Over the next few years he pushed Westminster for further devolution culminating in a referendum in September 2014 when the Scots voted to stay within the United Kingdom by 55 to 45 percent. With the Scotland Bill poised to give more power, the SNP had a remarkable landslide victory at the May 2015 general election, returning 56 out of 59 Scottish seats under the leadership of the charismatic Nicola Sturgeon. Whether Scotland finally opts for independence in a future referendum or the union remains intact, but with further devolutionary powers, hangs in the balance.

HISTORICAL LANDMARKS

c. 6000 BC First signs of human settlement in Scotland.

AD 84 Romans beat the 'Caledonians' in the Battle of Mons Graupius.

AD 185 Romans withdraw behind the line marked by Hadrian's Wall.

5th century Gaelic-speaking 'Scots' enter the country from Ireland.

563 St Columba spreads Christianity in Scotland.

775–800 Norse forces occupy Hebrides, Orkney and Shetland.

843 Kenneth MacAlpin becomes the first King of the Scots.

1290 A succession crisis allows Edward I of England to seize control.

1296 The Sacred Stone of Destiny is removed to London.

1297 William Wallace leads a revolt.

1305 Wallace taken to London and executed.

1306–28 Robert the Bruce wins independence back for Scotland.

1371 Reign of the Stewart dynasty begins.

1513 Defeat to the English in the Battle of Flodden, King James IV killed.

1542 Mary, Queen of Scots crowned at just six days old.

1561 Mary returns to Scotland from France to assume her throne.

1568 Mary flees to England, where she is imprisoned.

1587 Mary is beheaded in England.

1603 James VI, Mary's son, unites the thrones as James I of England.

1638 National Covenant signed, starting a long period of rebellion.

1707 Act of Union between England and Scotland.

1745 'Bonnie Prince Charlie' takes back Scotland and invades England.

1750–1800 'Scottish Enlightenment'.

1765 James Watt invents the steam engine.

1780 Crofters lose their land in the Highland Clearances programme.

1997 Referendum votes in favour of separate Scottish Parliament.

2004 New Scottish Parliament building opened.

2007 Alex Salmond (SNP) is elected First Minister of Scotland.

2014 Scotland votes to stay within the United Kingdom.

2015 The Scotland Bill is passed promising further devolution; the SNP has a landslide victory in the general election.

WHERE TO GO

Scotland's spectacular and varied scenery and rich historical heritage make it a fascinating country to explore. The country is about 565km (350 miles) from north to south and stretches in some parts as wide as 258km (160 miles), not counting the many islands of the Inner and Outer Hebrides. It is best to concentrate on a few areas, unless your time is unlimited. Scotland has a good network of roads in the Border country and motorways connecting major cities; however, the many winding roads in central Scotland and the single-lane roads in the Highlands can be slow going (see page 118). It's easy to explore Scotland via its excellent bus system (see page 132) or on one of the many tours to places of interest (see page 123).

In a country so rich in sights and experiences, only a selection can be presented below, but you'll find worthwhile sights, unspoiled villages, and spectacular scenery wherever you go, as well as plenty of chances for outdoor sports and adventure.

EDINBURGH

The ancient, proud capital of Scotland is, of course, at its most lively during the Edinburgh Festival in August, but all year round it provides many sights and entertainments to enjoy – particularly when the sun is shining. Both the Old Town up against the rock of Edinburgh Castle and the New Town across the way are full of impressive architecture. And you'll find a remarkably congenial atmosphere – an unexpected bonus in a city of just under half a million people.

Edinburgh's seven hills ❶ look northward over the great Firth of Forth estuary or southward to gentle green countryside that rises into hills. Tour guides boast that Edinburgh is

Statue of Greyfriars Bobby on Candlemaker Row

probably 1,500 years old and certainly it has been the capital of Scotland since 1437.

Despite all the echoes of the past, the city today seems decidedly young and vibrant. Most of the city's principal sights are within easy walking distance of each other or can be reached by public bus.

EDINBURGH CASTLE

Edinburgh's landmark and Scotland's most popular tourist attraction stands on an extinct volcano, high above the city. It is not known exactly how long ago the history of this great rock began, but there is archaeological evidence that there was human habitation here as early as the 9th century BC. A stone fortification was definitely erected late in the 6th century AD and the first proper castle was built in the 11th century.

Edinburgh's elegant rooftops

The entrance to **Edinburgh Castle Ⓐ** (tel: 0131-225 9846; www.edinburghcastle.gov.uk; daily Apr–Sept 9.30am–6pm, Oct–Mar 9.30am–5pm) lies just beyond the Esplanade, which was once a site for the execution of witches, later a parade ground, and is now a car park and site of the famous **Military Tattoo**, performed during the annual **Edinburgh International Festival**.

The famous Military Tattoo

The black naval cannons poking through the ramparts inside the gate have never been fired, but you'll see the cannon that booms out over the city every day (except Sunday) at one o'clock.

Tiny **St Margaret's Chapel** is the oldest church in use in Scotland. Said to have been built by David I in the early 12th century in honour of his mother, it has survived assaults over the centuries that destroyed the other structures on Castle Rock. The chapel, which has been simply restored with a plain white interior, is kept decorated with flowers by Scotswomen named Margaret. Close by, in a niche overlooking the city, is the Cemetery for Soldiers' Dogs, with the tombs of regimental mascots.

Further up the hill in Palace Yard is the **Great Hall**, claiming the finest hammer-beam ceiling in Britain. Built in 1503, the oak timbers are joined together without a single nail, screw or bolt. It is here that Scotland's Parliament met for a century. In the **State Apartments** is Queen Mary's Room, the very small chamber in which Mary, Queen of Scots gave birth to James VI (later James I of England).

The castle's greatest treasures – the crown, sceptre and sword of Scotland and the Stone of Destiny – are in the **Crown Room**, reached through a series of rooms with displays detailing Scottish history. The rooms are often extremely crowded. On a busy day, more than 10,000 viewers file through here to see the oldest royal regalia in Europe. The gold-and-pearl crown was first used for the coronation of Robert the Bruce in 1306. It was altered in 1540, and Charles II wore it for the last time in 1651. The sword and sceptre were given to James IV by popes Alexander VI and Julius II. The **Stone of Destiny**, on which Scottish monarchs were traditionally crowned, was only returned to Scotland from captivity in Westminster Abbey in 1996; it had been carried away from Scone in 1296 by English king Edward I, as a symbol of his conquest of Scotland (see page 16).

In the back vault of the French prisons is kept **Mons Meg**, a stout cannon that was forged in Mons (hence the name) in the 15th century. The 6.6-ton monster ingloriously blew up 200 years later while firing a salute to the Duke of Albany and York.

EDINBURGH MILITARY TATTOO

In 1950 the city established a Military Tattoo at the same time as the Festival. The event features a highly polished show of military marching, pageantry, mock battles and horsemanship, accompanied by the sounds of pipe-and-drum bands from around the world. All this happens nightly (except Sunday) against the backdrop of the magnificently floodlit castle in an arena erected in the Esplanade.

Tickets (which sell out months in advance) can be bought from the ticket office at 33–34 Market Street (behind Waverley Station), or by phoning tel: 0131-225 1188 (credit cards only). They can also be bought online at www.edintattoo.co.uk.

THE ROYAL MILE

The Royal Mile runs along the ridge from Edinburgh Castle downhill to the royal Palace of Holyroodhouse. The **Old Town's** famous thoroughfare, its cobbles now mostly smoothed, is actually about 2km (1.2 miles) long (the Scottish mile was longer than the English). As it descends, the Royal Mile takes five names: Castlehill, Lawnmarket, High Street, Canongate and Abbey Strand.

The Royal Mile

In medieval times, this was Edinburgh's main drag. Enclosed by the city walls, the town grew upwards. Edinburghers delight in recounting how residents of the high tenements and narrow 'wynds' (alleys) used to toss slops from windows after a perfunctory shout of 'Gardyloo!' (the equivalent of 'garde à l'eau'). Today, it is lined with historic buildings, tourist shops, restaurants and pubs.

On Castlehill the **Camera Obscura** at the top of the **Outlook Tower** (www.camera-obscura.co.uk; daily Apr–Oct 9.30am–7pm, July–Aug 9am–9pm, Nov–Mar 10am–6pm) offers a fascinating 15-minute show – make sure to go when the weather is dry. After climbing the 98 steps to a darkened chamber, you can enjoy living panoramas of the city, projected on to a circular table-screen. From the rooftop you can view the city through telescopes.

Opposite the tower, in the **Scotch Whisky Experience** (www. scotchwhiskyexperience.co.uk; daily Sept–May 10am–5.30pm, June–Aug until 6pm), you will be transported (in a barrel) through the history of Scotland's 'water of life'.

Further along, in James Court, Dr Samuel Johnson once visited his biographer, James Boswell, a native of Edinburgh. In Brodie's Close the popular local story of Deacon Brodie is recalled: a respected city official and carpenter by day, he was a burglar by night (he made wax impressions of his clients' house keys). Finally arrested and condemned, he tried to escape death by wearing a steel collar under his shirt. Unfortunately for him, the gallows, which he himself had designed, worked perfectly. His double life inspired fellow Scot Robert Louis Stevenson to write *Dr Jekyll and Mr Hyde*.

Gladstone's Land (477B Lawnmarket; www.nts.org.uk; daily Apr–Oct 10am–5pm, July–Aug until 6.30pm) is a 17th-century merchant's house, furnished in its original style, with a reconstructed shop booth on the ground floor.

A brief detour down George IV Bridge takes you to the statuette of **Greyfriars Bobby**. This Skye terrier allegedly waited by

The impressive interior of the National Museum of Scotland

his master's grave in nearby Greyfriars Churchyard for 14 years until dying of old age in 1872. Admiring the dog's fidelity, the authorities made Bobby a freeman of the city.

Across the road in Chambers Street stands the **National Museum of Scotland**  (www.nms.ac.uk; daily 10am–5pm; free), resplendent following the restoration of the old Royal Museum building. The National Museum pays homage to Scotland and its history, as well as ethnography, archaeology, technology and the decorative arts. New galleries devoted to science, technology and design are due to open in 2016.

Window designed by Burne Jones, St Giles' Cathedral

Back along the Royal Mile, **St Giles Cathedral** (www.st gilescathedral.org.uk; May–Sept Mon–Fri 9am–7pm, Sat 9am–5pm, Sun 1–5pm, Oct–Apr Mon–Sat 9am–5pm, Sun 1–5pm; free, but donations suggested), the High Kirk of Scotland, dominates Parliament Square. Its famous tower spire was built in 1495 as a replica of the Scottish crown. The oldest elements of St Giles are the huge 12th-century pillars that support the spire, but there was probably a church on the site since 854. John Knox preached here; he is thought to be buried in the rear graveyard. The soaring Norman interior of St Giles is filled with memorials recalling the great moments of Scottish history. The stained glass in the church dates from 1883 up to modern times. Most beautiful is the **Thistle Chapel**: dating from 1911, it is ornately carved out of Scottish oak. You'll see a stall for the queen and princely seats for the 16 Knights of the Thistle, Scotland's oldest order of chivalry.

Across the street lie the **City Chambers**, designed by John Adam in the 1750s. Beneath them is Mary King's Close, one of the areas where, until the 18th century, people lived in crowded, unsanitary conditions that aided the spread of plague and disease.

Further down, **John Knox House**  (45 High Street; Mon–Sat 10am–6pm, also July–Aug Sun noon–6pm), dating from 1450, is the oldest house in the city. Most interesting is the unchanged top storey with its stencilled beams. It contains an excellent exhibit on the life of John Knox (1513–72), leader of the Scottish Reformation and one of the most important figures in Scottish history (see page 19). It is also home to the **Scottish Storytelling Centre**.

Across the High Street is the **Museum of Childhood** (www.edinburghmuseums.org.uk; Mon–Sat 10am–5pm, Sun noon–5pm; free), with a display of children's toys and games through the centuries. At Canongate Tolbooth, the **People's Story** (163 Canongate; www.edinburghmuseums.org.uk; Mon–Sat 10am–5pm, Sun during Aug noon–5pm; free) is a social history

John Knox House

museum, telling the stories of Edinburgh's ordinary people through reconstructions that capture the sounds, sights and smells of the past. Across the road is the **Museum of Edinburgh** (www.edinburgh museums.org.uk; Mon–Sat 10am–5pm, also Sun noon–5pm in Aug; free), presenting local history exhibits from pre-historic times to the present.

Inside the state-of-the-art Scottish Parliament at Holyrood

The royal **Palace of Holyroodhouse**  (www.royalcollection. org.uk; daily Apr–Oct 9.30am–6pm, Nov–Mar 9.30am–4.30pm; closed for Royal and State visits), at the end of the Royal Mile, began life in about 1500 as a mere guest house for the adjacent, now-ruined abbey. It was much expanded and rebuilt in the 17th century. Visiting monarchs have often resided here (see page 19).

The long Picture Gallery showcases many portraits, purportedly of Scottish kings, which were dashed off between 1684–6 by Jacob de Wit the Younger, a Dutchman. In King James' Tower, up a winding inner stairway, are the apartments of Darnley and Mary, Queen of Scots. A plaque marks the spot where the Rizzio, Mary's Italian secretary, was stabbed with a dagger more than 56 times before the queen's eyes.

Above Holyroodhouse looms **Arthur's Seat** ; you can climb up to it through Holyrood Park. Back on Holyrood Road, you'll see the **Scottish Parliament building**  (www.scottish.parliament. uk; open Mon–Sat subject to Parliamentary business; tours

The Scott Monument

free), a magnificent showpiece designed by the Catalan architect Enric Miralles. Nearby, also on Holyrood Road, is **Our Dynamic Earth** (www.dynamicearth.co.uk; Apr–Oct daily 10am–5.30pm, July–Aug until 6pm, Nov–Mar Wed–Sun 10am–5.30pm), a permanent exhibition with displays on the formation and evolution of the planet.

NEW TOWN

Until late in the 18th century Edinburgh was confined to the crowded, unhealthy Old Town, along the ridge from the castle or in the wynds beneath the Royal Mile. The population, which numbered about 25,000 in 1700, had nearly tripled by 1767, when James Craig won a planning competition for an extension to the city. With significant help from the noted Robert Adam, he created the **New Town**, a complete complex of Georgian architecture.

At the centre of New Town is Edinburgh's main thoroughfare, bustling **Princes Street**. Between the historic Balmoral Hotel and Waverley Bridge is the three-level Princes Mall, with the tourist information office at street level. **Princes Street Gardens**, the city's green centrepiece, replaced what was once a fetid stretch of water called Nor' Loch. Rising from the gardens is the Gothic spire of the **Scott Monument**, which was erected in 1844 and has a statue of Sir Walter with his dog and statuettes of Scott's literary characters at its base. The gardens' famous **floral clock** is planted with some 24,000 flowers.

A sloping road known as the Mound passes through the gardens. Here, behind the Royal Scottish Academy, is the **Scottish National Gallery**  (www.nationalgalleries.org; daily 10am–6pm, Thu until 7pm; free) a small but distinguished collection. Look for Van Dyck's *Lomellini Family*, Rubens' *The Feast of Herod*, Velázquez's *Old Woman Cooking Eggs*, and a fine Rembrandt self-portrait. The English school is represented by Reynolds, Turner and Gainsborough. Don't miss the many paintings by the city's own Henry Raeburn, especially his well-known work, the *Rev. Robert Walker Skating on Duddingston Loch*.

At the west end of Princes Street is **Charlotte Square**, the neoclassical centrepiece of the New Town, designed in 1792 by Robert Adam, Scotland's most celebrated architect of the 18th century. The 11 houses on the north side of the square with their symmetrical facades are considered to be his finest work. At No. 7 Charlotte Square, **Georgian House** (www.nts.org.uk; daily Apr–Oct 10am–5pm, July–Aug until 6pm, Mar, Nov–Dec 11am–4pm) has been restored in period-style by the National Trust for Scotland. In the dining room is a splendid table setting of Wedgwood and Sheffield silver cutlery, and in the bed-chamber a marvellous medicine chest as well as a 19th-century water closet called 'the receiver'.

National Gallery

Calton Hill offers panoramic views of the city

The excellent **Scottish National Gallery of Modern Art** (75 Belford Road; www.nationalgalleries.org; daily 10am–5pm, Aug until 6pm; free) is well worth a visit. Scotland's national collection of modern and contemporary art is housed in two neo-classical buildings, Modern One and Modern Two, set in parkland dotted with sculptures by important artists such as Henry Moore. The gallery has an international collection as well as work by Scottish artists, and also hosts touring exhibits.

Along Inverleith Row extends the 30 hectares (75 acres) of the much-admired **Royal Botanic Garden** (www.rbge.org.uk; daily Mar–Sept 10am–6pm, Feb and Oct 10am–5pm, Nov–Jan 10am–4pm; gardens free, charge for glasshouses) with a huge collection of rhododendrons and a remarkable rock garden, as well as cavernous plant houses.

At the east end of Princes Street is **Calton Hill**, reached via Waterloo Place. Here you'll find the old City Observatory now home to the Collective Gallery, and from the top of the Nelson Monument there is a fine panoramic view.

On the waterfront at Leith the **Royal Yacht Britannia** (tel: 0131-555 5566; www.royalyachtbritannia.co.uk; daily July–Sept 9.30am–4.30pm, Apr–June and Oct until 4pm, Nov–Mar 10am–3.30pm) is docked.

EXCURSIONS IN LOTHIAN

From Edinburgh you can take several excursions by bus to points of interest in the countryside. One of the shortest is to the huge **Hopetoun House** near South Queensferry, 10 miles (16km) west of Edinburgh (www.hopetoun.co.uk; Apr–Sept daily 10.30am–5pm), a fine example of neoclassical 18th-century architecture. The house has fine original furnishings as well as paintings by Dutch and Italian masters and is set in 100 acres (41 hectares) of parkland with herds of red deer. Its gardens were designed in the grand style of Versailles.

Nearby at Linlithgow, overlooking the loch, stand the ruins of **Linlithgow Palace** (tel: 01506-842896; daily Apr–Sept 9.30am–5.30pm, Oct–Mar 9.30am–4.30pm), which was the birthplace of Mary, Queen of Scots in 1542. James V, Mary's father, gave the fountain in the courtyard to his wife Mary of Guise as a wedding present. The Great Hall measures 94ft (28m) in length and enough of the enormous building still stands for the visitor to imagine what life must have been like here.

Situated alongside is the **Church of St Michael**, one of the best medieval parish churches in Britain and a fine example of the Scottish Decorated style, where a

Forth Rail Bridge

About 8 miles (13km) west of Edinburgh is one of the Victorian era's greatest engineering feats, the Forth Rail Bridge. Completed in 1890, the bridge comprises three huge cantilevers joined by two suspended spans, for a total length of 4,746ft (1,447m). For many years it was the world's longest bridge.

ghost is said to have warned James IV not to fight against England shortly before he and so many Scots were killed at the Battle of Flodden.

Golf courses, beaches, and pleasant villages make East Lothian a popular holiday destination. A pleasant coastal walk connects North Berwick and Gullane Bay. At **Dirleton**, you will find original stone cottages surrounding a large village green beneath a ruined castle. You can take a boat from North Berwick around the Bass Rock where you will see some of the 8,000 gannets which easily outnumber the other inhabitants such as puffins, shags, kittiwakes and cormorants.

Near Seacliff beach are the formidable reddish ruins of 600-year-old **Tantallon Castle** (daily Apr–Sept 9.30am–5.30pm, Oct–Mar 9.30am–4.30pm) high up on a cliff. Queen Victoria visited this fortress of the Black Douglas clan in 1898, and probably peered into the well, cut 89ft (27m) through sheer rock.

In the Pentland Hills, just south of Edinburgh, **Rosslyn Chapel ❷** (www.rosslynchapel.org.uk; Mon–Sat 9.30am–5pm, Sun noon–4.45pm) in Roslin, Midlothian, is an unusual

THE APPRENTICE

Contained within the small, 15th-century Rosslyn Chapel is the most elaborate stone carving in Scotland. The Seven Deadly Sins, the Seven Cardinal Virtues and a dance of death are extravagantly represented in bas-relief, although interest tends to focus on the Apprentice Pillar with its intricate and abundant flowers and foliage.

The story has never been authenticated, but the pillar is said to have been carved by an apprentice while his master was away. The work was so fine that the master, on his return, flew into a jealous rage and killed the apprentice. Three carved heads at the end of the nave are alleged to depict the unfortunate youth, his grieving mother and his master.

church. Built in 1446, it is richly decorated with carvings both pagan and Christian – biblical stories, 'green men', references to the Knights Templar, and plants of the New World that predate Columbus's voyage of discovery.

Abbotsford House

SOUTHERN SCOTLAND

The many ruined castles and abbeys bear silent witness to the turbulent history of the Borders and Galloway area – centuries of conflict between the Scots and the English and also between Scots and Scots. Today this is a region of peaceful countryside, packed with literary associations, with historic houses, tranquil rivers and attractive market towns.

THE BORDERS

Rolling green hills, woods and farmland run from Lothian into Scotland's Borders region. The hilly countryside around **Peebles** ❸ is worth exploring, particularly the beautiful Manor Valley. Nearby there are two quite outstanding gardens: **Kailzie Gardens** (on B7062 southeast of Peebles) and **Dawyck Botanic Gardens** (on B712 southwest).

To the east along the River Tweed, near Innerleithen, is **Traquair House** (www.traquair.co.uk; daily Apr–Sept 11am–5pm, Oct 11am–4pm, Nov Sat–Sun only 11am–3pm), dating back some 1,000 years. In all, 27 Scottish and English kings

have stayed here. It also sheltered Catholic priests and sup-
porters of the Jacobite cause, and is full of curiosities like a
secret stairway to a priest's room and a 14th-century hand-
printed bible. It is the oldest inhabited house in Scotland.

Abbotsford House (www.scottsabbotsford.com; daily Apr–
Sept 10am–5pm, Mar and Oct–Nov 10am–4pm; visitor centre
open all year), further down the Tweed, past Galashiels, was
the home of **Sir Walter Scott**. He spent the last 20 years of
his life here, writing frantically in an effort to pay his debts.
Visitors may inspect rooms containing his personal belong-
ings and collection of arms and armour.

THE BORDER ABBEYS

The **Border abbeys** were all founded in the 12th century during the reign of David I. Scotland's four great southern monasteries stand in varying degrees of ruin today. All are worth
a visit. Always vulnerable to invading forces from England,
the abbeys endured frequent sacking, restoration, then new
destruction, again and again.

The impressive ruins of **Melrose Abbey** (daily 9.30am–
5.30pm, Oct–Mar until 4.30pm), built of rose-coloured stone,
are set off by close-trimmed lawns. You can still see part of
the original, high-arching stone church. You will find a small visitor centre and a museum crowded with relics opposite the entrance.

Kelso Abbey was founded in 1128 and took 84 years to complete. Just one arcaded transept tower and a facade are all that remain to suggest the original dimensions of the

Melrose Abbey

The destruction caused by Edward II's attack on Melrose Abbey in 1322 prompted Robert the Bruce to fund the abbey's restoration. His heart is said to be buried near the abbey's high altar, but subsequent excavations have failed to locate any trace of it.

oldest and once the richest southern Scottish monastery.

Closer to the English border on the River Tweed, **Jedburgh Abbey** ❹ (daily 9.30am–5.30pm, Oct–Mar until 4.30pm) is a more complete structure. The main aisle of the church, which is lined by a three-tiered series of nine arches, is nearly intact. There is an informative visitor centre and a museum. Also in Jedburgh is **Mary, Queen of Scots' Visitor Centre** (Mar–Nov Mon–Sat 10am–4.30pm, Sun noon–4pm; free). The house was built around 1500 and was

Dryburgh Abbey ruins

named after the queen following a visit in 1566. The centre contains exhibits including the queen's death warrant and a death mask made just after her execution in 1587.

Dryburgh Abbey (daily 9.30am–5.30pm, Oct–Mar until 4.30pm) is probably the most beautiful of the four abbeys, and sits among stately beeches and cedars on the banks of the River Tweed. Some of the monks' cloister survives, but little now remains of the church. The grave of Sir Walter Scott can be found here.

From Bemersyde Hill, which is reached from Dryburgh via Gattonside along a beautiful tree-tunnelled road (B6356), you can enjoy **Scott's View**, a panorama of the three peaks of the Eildon Hills and the writer Sir Walter Scott's favourite scenic spot.

AYRSHIRE, DUMFRIES AND GALLOWAY

Ayrshire is **Burns Country**. Robert Burns, the national poet of Scotland, was born in 1759 in Alloway, just south of the thriving coastal town of Ayr, and he lived in this area most of his very full 37 years. Here are all the echoes of his narrative poem 'Tam o'Shanter' and the 'Auld Brig o' Doon' which has spanned the River Doon in Alloway for 700 years. Burns' liking for his wee dram and bonnie lassies seems to have enhanced his already monumental reputation.

In Alloway you can visit the **Burns National Heritage Park** ❺ (tel: 01292-443700; www.burnsmuseum.org.uk), with his carefully preserved birthplace, **Burns Cottage** (daily Apr–Sept 10am–5.30pm, Oct–Mar 10am–4pm). In this whitewashed cottage with a thatched roof you'll see the box bed where Burns and three of his brothers used to sleep as children; even his razor and shaving mirror are displayed. The park also features the award-winning **Robert Burns Birthplace Museum** (same hours as Burns Cottage), devoted to the life and times of the iconic poet, the Alloway Auld Kirk, the setting for Burn's Tam O' Shanter, and the Burns Monument and gardens.

You can follow the **Burns Heritage Trail** down to Dumfries where he died in 1796. The Burns Centre in Dumfries focuses on the years he lived in the town; he is buried in a mausoleum in St Michael's Churchyard.

Burns National Heritage Park

It is well worth making a detour to visit 17th-century **Drumlanrig Castle** (www.drumlanrigcastle.co.uk; grounds: Apr–Sept daily 10am–5pm; castle: July–Aug

The Brig o' Doon features in Burns' poetry

daily 11am–5pm, regular guided tours) near Thornhill. Of all the priceless treasures in this pink sandstone mansion, you'll linger longest over Rembrandt's *Old Woman Reading* on the main stairway; there are also paintings by Holbein and Gainsborough. Napoleon's dispatch box is also here, a gift from Wellington to the owner of the castle, as well as relics of Bonnie Prince Charlie (see page 21).

South of Dumfries you will find the lovely red sandstone ruins of **Sweetheart Abbey** (Apr–Sept daily 9.30am–5.30pm, Oct–Mar Sat–Wed 9.30am–4.30pm), which was founded in the 13th century by the pious (and rich) Devorgilla Balliol, Lady of Galloway. She dedicated it to her husband, John Balliol, who died at a young age and whose embalmed heart she carried around with her in a silver box until her own death in 1289. Also south of Dumfries, do not miss the moated fairytale **Caerlaverock Castle** with red sandstone walls which was built around 1270.

On the other side of the River Nith, **Ruthwell Cross**, named after its hamlet, is kept in a pretty church surrounded by

Gretna Green

Just over the border from England is the small town of Gretna Green, which became celebrated for celebrating marriages. It was the first available community where eloping couples from England could take advantage of Scotland's different marriage laws. Many a makeshift ceremony was performed at the Old Blacksmith's, now a visitor centre, and many romantic couples still choose to be married at Gretna Green today.

weathered tombstones. This great monument was carved out of brownish-pink stone some 1,300 years ago. Standing 18ft (5.5m) high, it is covered with sculpted figures and runic inscriptions. If the church is locked the key is in a box at the manse next door.

Southwest Scotland has beautiful shorelines, moors and forest scenery. It also claims milder weather than any other area. Just north of Newton Stewart is **Galloway Forest Park**, where you can walk through wild hill country. To the extreme southwest is the peninsula called the Rhinns of Galloway. The **Logan Botanic Garden** (mid-Mar–Oct daily 10am–5pm) has Scotland's best collection of tree ferns and, among many palms and other warm-weather species, superb magnolias from western China.

South of the gardens is the most southerly point in Scotland, the high-cliffed Mull of Galloway, where you can see the Isle of Man on a clear day.

On a pastoral hill midway up the peninsula is a stone chapel which contains several of Scotland's oldest Christian relics: the **Kirkmadrine Stones**, which consist of three stones and various fragments dating back to the 5th century.

CULZEAN CASTLE

One of Scotland's top attractions, **Culzean Castle ❻** (www. nts.org.uk; daily Mar–Oct 10.30am–5pm, guided tours daily

11am and 2.30pm; country park daily year-round 9.30am–sunset) towers above the sea on a rugged stretch of the Ayrshire coast. It stands in an estate of over 500 acres (202 hectares) of parkland and stately formal gardens. Now a National Trust property, the castle dates mostly from the late 18th century when it was transformed for the Kennedy family from a 16th-century tower house by the architect Robert Adam. The oval staircase is considered one of Adam's finest designs; the best room is the circular drawing room with its ceiling in three pastel shades, a perfect example of Scottish Enlightenment, its windows overlooking the waves of the Firth of Clyde breaking on the rocks 151ft (46m) below. The grounds have much to offer, from the Fountain Court with its orangery and terraces to the walled garden with a stone grotto and fruit-filled greenhouses and the quirky follies dotted around the estate. In the summer on Sunday afternoons, a pipe band performs on the large sunken lawn of the Fountain Court just below the castle.

Culzean Castle

ARRAN

The unspoilt **Isle of Arran** ❼ in the Firth of Clyde has been called 'Scotland in miniature'. Car ferries ply regularly between Arran's capital, Brodick, and Ardrossan on the Ayrshire coast; the

Glen Rosa, Arran

journey takes 55 minutes. In summer a smaller ferry links northern Arran to Claonaig in Argyll; in winter it links to Tartbet (Loch Fyne). Brodick village nestles on a bay in the shadow of **Goatfell**, which, at 2,867ft (874m), is the highest peak on Arran. On Brodick Bay, **Brodick Castle** (www.nts.org.uk; daily May–Sept 11am–4pm, Apr and Oct 11am–3pm; country park open daily year-round 9.30am–sunset), containing a wealth of treasures, is surrounded by magnificent gardens.

Red deer roam the island's beautiful mountain glens and can often be seen in North Glen Sannox between Lochranza and Sannox. Arran is above all an island for hill walkers or climbers. The most dramatic scenery is in the north of the island. There are ten summits over 2,000ft (610m) and dozens of ridge routes. In the south the topography is gentler, with pleasant hills around the villages of Lamlash and Whiting Bay.

Among the hundred or so species of birds known to frequent Arran are peregrine falcons and rare golden eagles. Seals like the rocks around Arran's 56 miles (90km) of coast. In addition, basking sharks can be seen offshore in the summer.

Arran has some outstanding archaeological sites. There are Neolithic chamber tombs, such as the one at **Torrylinn**, near Lagg, and Bronze Age stone circles around Machrie on the west coast. Towards the island's southwest corner on a wild, cliff-backed coast are the **King's Caves**, where Robert the Bruce is said to have taken refuge in 1307. The caves are a 20-minute walk from the car park.

GLASGOW

Be prepared for a pleasant surprise. In recent years, **Glasgow** ❽ has undergone major changes, and has not only cleaned its splendid Victorian buildings and generally polished up its act, but now proudly presents itself as one of Europe's major centres for culture and the arts. The city is home to the Scottish Opera, Scottish Ballet, the Royal Scottish National Orchestra and the BBC Scottish Symphony Orchestra, and it stages an annual comedy festival in March, as well as a jazz festival in June.

At the heart of Glasgow lies **George Square**, overlooked by the impressive **City Chambers**, opened by Queen Victoria in 1888 (a statue of her on horseback is on the west side of the square). Free tours are given Mon–Fri at 10.30am and 2.30pm. On the south side at No. 11 is a tourist information centre. Glasgow's sophisticated main shopping area is the Buchanan Quarter, which is a block northwest of George Square.

TRACES OF MACKINTOSH

Glasgow Stock Exchange

The city is closely connected with Scottish architect **Charles Rennie Mackintosh**. Almost forgotten by his native city at the time of his death, he has become world famous, and today his unique vision is a prominent feature of Glasgow's art scene. The **Glasgow School of Art** (www.

gsa.ac.uk; tel: 0141-353 4256; 167 Renfew Street; tours given daily at 11am, 2pm and 3.15pm, also 11.30am July–mid-Sept; reservations recommended), was seriously damaged by fire in 2014 and is due to undergo restoration. The Mackintosh at the GSA Tour can be taken from the visitor centre opposite the damaged building.

Opened in 1996, the **House for an Art Lover** (Bellahouston Park; www.houseforanartlover.co.uk; times vary, check website for details; café and shop open daily 10am–5pm) was created from a portfolio Mackintosh submitted for a design competition in 1901, following a brief to 'design a house in a thoroughly modern style, where one can be lavishly entertained'.

There is also an exhibit on Mackintosh at **The Lighthouse**, on Mitchell Lane, and the evocative rooms of Mackintosh's own house have been preserved in the **Hunterian Museum and**

THE GLASGOW BOYS

The late-19th and early-20th centuries were a time of artistic ferment in Glasgow, but because of the hide-bound local arts establishment, Glasgow artists often had to look for recognition outside Scotland. Charles Rennie Mackintosh was a leading figure in the Art Nouveau movement on the continent, and influenced designers such as Frank Lloyd Wright as far afield as Chicago, but was not admired at home.

Others who suffered the same fate were painters Sir James Guthrie, Robert MacGregor, William Kennedy, Sir John Lavery and Edward Arthur Walton. After a successful London exhibition, the 'Glasgow School' was born, but the artists always called themselves the 'Glasgow Boys'. More recently, a new generation of Glasgow Boys began to emerge from the School of Art in the 1970s and 1980s. The works of Glasgow Boys of both generations can be seen in the Kelvingrove Art Gallery and the Gallery of Modern Art on Queen Street.

Art Gallery  at Glasgow University (www.gla.ac.uk/hunterian; Tue–Sat 10am–5pm; free, charge for special exhibitions). On Sauchiehall Street, stop off at No. 217 for the **Willow Tea Rooms** (tel: 0141-332 0521; www.willowtearooms.co.uk; Mon–Sat 9.30am–5.30pm, Sun 10.30am–5.30pm, last orders 4.30pm), a survivor of a series of tearooms designed by the architect. For more information on Mackinstosh

Burrell Collection

attractions in the city contact the Charles Rennie Mackintosh Society (tel: 0141-946 6600; www.crmsociety.com).

MAJOR MUSEUMS

Glasgow's most important museum is the **Burrell Collection**  (www.glasgowlife.org.uk/museums; 2060 Pollokshaws Road; Mon–Thu and Sat 10am–5pm, Fri and Sun 11am–5pm; free) in Pollok Country Park to the southwest of the city centre. Opened in 1983, it holds the thousands of pieces amassed by shipping tycoon Sir William Burrell. The collection has everything from ancient Greek statues to Impressionist paintings, medieval tapestries to stained glass. Also in the park is Pollok House with a fine collection of Spanish art.

In Kelvingrove Park is the city's splendid **Art Gallery and Museum** (Argyle Street; www.glasgowlife.org.uk/museums; Mon–Thu and Sat 10am–5pm, Fri and Sun 11am–5pm; free). On display are a collection of 17th-century Dutch paintings, including Rembrandt's masterpiece *A Man in Armour*, as well as some

SSE Hydro arena in Finnieston

French Impressionists, 19th-century Scottish paintings and works by the Glasgow Boys. Other highlights include the Charles Rennie Mackintosh and Glasgow Style Gallery and a living bee exhibition.

Also giving a fascinating look into Glasgow's past is the **Tenement House** (www.nts.org.uk; 145 Buccleuch Street; Apr–Oct daily 1–5pm). Miss Agnes Toward, who lived here from 1911 until 1965, never threw anything away, nor did she ever attempt to modernise the flat; the result is a fascinating glimpse into early 20th-century social history.

OLD GLASGOW

Cathedral Street, located northeast of the city centre, brings you to the city's fine **Cathedral ⓒ** (www.glasgowcathedral.org.uk; Apr–Sept Mon–Sat 9.30am–5.30pm, Sun 1–5pm, Oct–Mar Mon–Sat 9.30am–4.30pm, Sun 1–4.30pm; free), the only medieval cathedral in Scotland that has survived intact. Parts of it are almost 800 years old, and it has an unusual two-level construction. The lower church contains the tomb of St Mungo (Kentigern), the city's patron saint. Above the church is the **Necropolis**, filled with the extravagant tombs of the city's late, great Victorians.

Across the street is **Provand's Lordship ⓓ** (www.glasgowlife.org.uk/museums; daily Tue–Thu and Sat 10am–5pm,

Fri and Sun 11am–5pm; free), the oldest house in Glasgow. Originally, the 15th-century house was home to the cathedral administrative clergy. With its thick stone walls, it is a rare example of Scottish domestic architecture. Opposite is **St Mungo Museum of Religious Life and Art** (Tue–Thu and Sat 10am–5pm, Fri and Sun 11am–5pm; free).

Head south down High Street to London Road to reach **Glasgow Green**, one of the city's many public parks and the oldest in Britain. Here you can learn about the working life of Glaswegians throughout history in the **People's Palace** (www.glasgowlife.org.uk/museums; Tue–Thu and Sat 10am–5pm, Fri and Sun 11am–5pm; free). The nearby Barras indoor market, open weekends, will give you the chance to rub shoulders with local people and perhaps even pick up a bargain or two.

THE OLD DOCKS

More contemporary developments can be seen by the old docks to the west of the city centre. On the north bank of the Clyde is the **Scottish Exhibition and Conference Centre**, its distinctive 'Armadillo' building designed by Sir Norman Foster. Almost opposite, on the south bank, is the stunning, titanium-clad **Glasgow Science Centre ❼** (www.glasgow sciencecentre.org; daily 10am–5pm). This comprises three separate buildings: the Science Mall which contains educational exhibits and a planetarium; the revolving 120ft (400m) Glasgow Tower with views as far as Ben Lomond; and an IMAX cinema. To the west, beyond Stobcross Quay and adjacent to Glasgow Harbour, the futuristic interactive **Riverside Museum** (www.glasgowlife.org.uk/museums; Mon–Thu and Sat 10am–5pm, Fri and Sun 11am–5pm; free) is dedicated to transport. The Tall Ship, a three-masted Clyde-built barque from 1896, is moored nearby.

Stirling Castle

CENTRAL SCOTLAND

STIRLING

With its proud Renaissance castle commanding the major route between the Lowlands and the Highlands, **Stirling** ❾ for centuries saw much of Scotland's worst warfare. Guides at the castle regale visitors with tales of sieges, intrigue, dastardly murders and atrocities, and an audio-visual presentation just off the castle esplanade brings the savage saga vividly to life. In contrast to sober Edinburgh Castle, **Stirling Castle** (www.stirlingcastle.gov.uk; daily 9.30am–6pm, Oct–Mar until 5pm) has a facade covered with all sorts of carvings. Most of the castle dates back about 500 years, though the rock was fortified at least four centuries earlier. The **Palace** was built by James V in Renaissance style, and of interest here are the Stirling Heads, carved roundels that are possibly portraits of members of the court. Mary, Queen of Scots spent her early childhood here, and she was crowned as an infant in the **Chapel Royal**. The **Great Hall**, which faces the upper square, was once the greatest medieval chamber in Scotland, suitable for holding sessions of Parliament, but it later suffered through two centuries of use as a military barracks. Restoration has returned it to its original grandeur. The Museum of the Argyll and Sutherland Highlanders contains banners, regimental silver, and artefacts that go back to the Battle of Waterloo. A statue of Robert the Bruce is on the Esplanade.

Seven battlefields can be seen from the castle. In 1297, William Wallace defeated the English at Stirling Bridge. The **Wallace Monument** is at Abbey Craig, east of the town centre. The battlefield of **Bannockburn** is visible to the south of the castle. Here you'll find the **Battle of Bannockburn Experience** (www.battleofbannockburn.com; daily Mar–Oct 10am–5.30pm, Jan–Feb and Nov–Dec 10am–5pm), where the National Trust presents a 3-D visual show (booking essential) bringing to life Robert the Bruce's epic victory over the English in 1314. Commemorating this triumph is an

THE FALKIRK WHEEL

In 2002 Scotland re-asserted itself in the world of engineering by unveiling an iconic landmark, the Falkirk Wheel. Named after the nearby town in central Scotland, the wheel is the world's only rotating boat lift. Built at a cost of over £17 million, the structure connects the Forth and Clyde Canal to the Union Canal, re-establishing the link between Edinburgh and Glasgow. It is part of a larger project to restore the waterways between the east and west coasts.

The site includes a visitor's centre containing a shop, café and exhibition centre (www.thefalkirkwheel.co.uk; daily Mar–Oct 10am–5.30pm; free, charge for boat trips; café and shop open year-round).

equestrian statue of **Robert the Bruce** with the inscription of his declaration: 'We fight not for glory nor for wealth nor for honour, but only and alone we fight for freedom, which no good man surrenders but with his life'.

The medieval **Church of the Holy Rude** (St John Street, Castle Wynd; May–Sept daily 11am–4pm; admission by donation) has a notable medieval hammerbeam oak roof. The infant James VI was crowned here in 1567.

Just north of Stirling, 700-year-old **Dunblane Cathedral** is one of the finest examples of Gothic church architecture in Scotland. It is about a century older than **Doune Castle** (daily Apr–Sept 9.30am–5.30pm, Oct–Mar 9.30am–4.30pm) just to the west. A fortress-residence and once a Stuart stronghold, it is one of the best preserved castles of its period. It has a central courtyard and Great Hall with an open-timbered roof and a minstrel's gallery.

LOCH LOMOND AND THE TROSSACHS

Romantically connected with the legend of Rob Roy, Scotland's folk hero, the **Trossachs** is a region of lovely lochs, glens and bens (mountain peaks), and craggy hills. 'Trossachs' probably means 'bristly places', after the area's wooded crags. Loch Lomond and the Trossachs National Park opened in 2002. Callander is a good centre from which to explore the Trossachs; information is available at the Rob Roy Visitor Centre. You can take a cruise on **Loch Katrine**, the setting of Sir Walter Scott's poem *The Lady of the Lake*, on the Victorian steamer *Sir Walter Scott*, which leaves from Trossachs Pier. Salmon may well be leaping up the easily accessible Falls of Leny below Loch Lubnaig. Between Callander and Aberfoyle, the Duke's Pass has some fine views. To the south is the **Queen Elizabeth Forest Park**, whose woodland walks offer a chance to spot wildlife.

Loch Lomond , the largest freshwater expanse in Great Britain, runs about 24 miles (39km) north to south. Ben Lomond (3,192ft/973m) and companion peaks look down on the sometimes choppy water at the north end of the loch, while to the south the landscape is tranquil and rolling. **Luss** is the prettiest of the little lochside villages. In **Balloch**, stop at the Lomond Shores, Sea Life Aquarium and National Park Visitor Centre. A number of cruises set sail on Loch Lomond from Balloch, Tarbet, and Luss. The West Highland Way provides a scenic footpath along the east bank of Loch Lomond.

To the west of Loch Lomond at the northern end of Loch Fyne, **Inveraray Castle** (www.inveraray-castle.com; daily Apr–Oct 10am–5.45pm), with its pointed turrets and Gothic design, contains a wealth of treasures. Home of the Dukes of Argyll, it has been the headquarters of Clan Campbell

Loch Lomond

(called 'uncrowned kings of the Highlands') since the 15th century, although the present building dates only from between 1740 and 1790. The impressive interior holds a collection of Regency furniture; Chinese porcelain; portraits by Gainsborough, Ramsey, and Raeburn; and an armoury with an amazing array of broadswords, Highland rifles, and medieval halberds. The guides point out with pride the portrait of the sixth duke, said both to have gambled away a fortune and to have fathered 398 illegitimate children.

Further south along Loch Fyne are the delightful **Crarae Garden** ⓫ (daily 9.30am–sunset), with many unusual plants, such as the Himalayan rhododendrons, and plants from Tasmania and New Zealand. The gardens are at their best in late spring. You can choose from several walks over the 50 acres (20 hectares) of hillside, all within earshot of a plunging brook.

FIFE

Dunfermline is dominated by the ruins of the **Abbey and Palace of Dunfermline**. King Malcolm Canmore made Dunfermline his capital around 1060, and his pious queen, St Margaret, founded the Benedictine abbey. Of the great abbey church, only the nave with its massive Norman arches survives. Nearby, the 14th-century **Abbot House** has an interesting historical display. Industrialist and philanthropist Andrew Carnegie was born here and his birthplace cottage and museum is open to visitors (www.carnegiebirthplace.com; Mar–Nov Mon–Sat 10am–5pm, Sun 2–5pm; free).

Also in this area is **Culross**, thought to be the birthplace of St Mungo. It is a wonderfully preserved 17th- and 18th-century village restored by the National Trust for Scotland.

Among places of historic interest are Bruce's Palace from 1577 and the ruined abbey and Abbey House. The Trust runs guided tours departing from the palace reception.

The most famous place on the Fife coast is **St Andrews** , where golf has been played for 500 years. It's possible, if you are an experienced golfer, to tee off on the **Old Course** (see page 89). At the 18th hole is the Royal and Ancient Golf Club, which maintains the rules of the game. This pleasant seaside resort is also home to Scotland's oldest university (founded in 1413); its buildings are dotted all over town. Here also is the ruin of what was Scotland's largest-ever cathedral, an enormous structure built in the 12th and 13th centuries, where the marriage of James V and Mary of Guise took place. Learn more about golf at the **British Golf Museum** (www.britishgolfmuseum.com); and for culture the local theatre, The Byre, is well-regarded.

St Andrews' famous golf course

The picturesque **East Neuk** fishing villages on Fife's southeastern coast are more dependent on tourism than fishing nowadays. **Crail** is a little port with a Dutch-style tolbooth (court-house jail) and restored buildings: a photographer's delight. **Anstruther** (which the locals pronounce 'Anster'), once the herring capital of Scotland, is worth a stop for the Scottish Fisheries Museum (www.scotfishmuseum.org) with its realistic fisherman's cottage of about 1900, magnificent ship models, whale tusks, and a display about trawlers. From here you can go to the **Isle of May**, a bird sanctuary with cliffs that measure 249ft (76m). **Pittenweem's** venerable harbour is still the base for what's left of the East Neuk fishing fleet, which specialises in prawn fishing.

The RRS Discovery

Across the Firth of Tay, which is spanned by one of the world's longest railway bridges as well as a road bridge, lies **Dundee**, famous maritime and industrial centre. Docked in the harbour is the Royal Navy's oldest ship, HMS *Unicorn*, and Captain Scott's ship, the RRS *Discovery*, built here at the turn of the 20th century and used in his polar expeditions.

PERTH AND SCONE PALACE

Perth ⑬ was Scotland's medieval capital, and has

many reminders of its historic heritage. John Knox preached in the **Church of St John**, founded in 1126, inspiring his followers to destroy many monasteries in the area in 1559. Just 2 miles (3km) north of Perth, the pale red sandstone **Scone Palace** (www.scone-palace.co.uk; daily Apr–Oct 9.30am–5pm, Nov–Mar grounds only Fri–Sun 10am–4pm) was built on the site of one of these mon-

> ### Three Js
>
> The industrial history of Dundee is often described by 'the three Js' – jute, jam and journalism. The city's rapid growth in population during the 19th century was due in large part to the jute industry, now completely gone. The only 'J' still thriving is journalism – newspaper and comic publisher D.C. Thomson & Co have been in busy for over a century.

asteries. From the 9th to the 13th century, Scone (pronounced 'Scoon') guarded the famous **Stone of Destiny**, on which the kings of the Scots were crowned. Edward I, believing in the symbolic magic of the stone, carried it away in 1296 and took it to London where, until 1996, it rested under the chair on which the English kings were crowned in Westminster Abbey. Romantics, however, believe that the stone, now on display in Edinburgh Castle (see page 30), is not the original stone, but a replica produced by the Scots to fool Edward, and suggest that the real stone (which they think was covered with carvings) is still hidden in Scotland.

In the palace, the ancestral home of the Earls of Mansfield, are many treasures, including early Sèvres, Derby, and Meissen porcelain, and artefacts such as the embroideries of Mary, Queen of Scots. In the Long Gallery are more than 80 Vernis Martin objects, which look like lacquered porcelain but are in fact papier mâché. This unique collection will never be copied: the Martin brothers died in Paris in the 18th century without disclosing the secret of their varnish. Before leaving Scone, stroll through the grounds to the Pinetum, an imposing collection of California sequoias, cedars, Norway spruces, silver firs, and other conifers in a gorgeous setting.

PERTHSHIRE

Glamis Castle (www.glamis-castle.co.uk; daily Apr–Oct 10am–5.30pm, last admission 4.30pm) lies northeast of Perth towards Forfar. It was the childhood home of Queen Elizabeth, the late Queen Mother, and the birthplace of the late Princess Margaret. Visitors can take guided tours through the magnificent rooms. On the way to Glamis Castle, enthusiasts of archaeology will want to stop to look at the elaborately carved early-Christian and Pictish monuments in the museum at **Meigle**.

Glamis Castle

Northwest of Perth is **Dunkeld**, with its restored 'little houses' from the 17th century. They lead to a once grand cathedral, now partly ruined, although the choir of the cathedral was renovated in the 17th century to serve as a parish church. The cathedral stands amid tall trees, lawns, and interesting gravestones beside the River Tay. The site was an ancient centre of Celtic Catholicism, and St Columba is said to have preached in a monastery on this site. Also note Thomas Telford's arched bridge (1809) over the Tay.

Binoculars are provided at a fine wooden hide at the **Loch of the Lowes Wildlife Reserve**, two wooded miles (3km) from Dunkeld. Here you can scan all kinds of water-bird life and study trees where ospreys nest after migrating from Africa.

At the hamlet of Meikleour, one of the arboreal wonders of the world lines the road: a

Pitlochry

gigantic **beech hedge**, which at about 100ft (30m) is the highest anywhere, planted in 1746 and still thriving.

Near Aberfeldy, once a Pictish centre, is the delightful little village of Fortingall on Loch Tay, with probably Scotland's finest thatched-roof cottages. It boasts the 'oldest living tree' in Europe, the **Fortingall Yew**, although there are other contenders. This ancient yew tree, surrounded by a rusty iron and stone enclosure in Fortingall's churchyard, is still growing and certainly doesn't look its presumed age – 3,000 years. The hamlet is in Glen Lyon, the 'longest, loveliest, loneliest' glen in Scotland, according to the locals. Tranquillity reigns. Tradition has it – without scholarly confirmation – that Pontius Pilate was born in a nearby military encampment while his father was a Roman emissary to the Pictish king in the area.

Centrally located, the crowded summer resort of **Pitlochry** ⓮ is surrounded by dozens of attractions, both scenic and manmade. In the town itself, you might visit the Pitlochry Dam and Fish Ladder, where each year between

Blair Castle, seat of the Earls and Dukes of Atholl

5,000 and 7,000 salmon are counted electronically and watched through a windowed chamber as they make their way towards their spawning grounds. Pitlochry also has a **Festival Theatre**.

A short drive west will bring you to the **Pass of Killiecrankie**, where you will want to walk along wooded paths to the spectacular parts of the gorge. A National Trust centre here describes a particularly bloody battle between Jacobite and government forces in 1689. Just south, a roadside promontory known as the **Queen's View** commands a glorious sweep down along Loch Tummel and over Highland hills. On a good day this is among the best panoramas in Scotland.

North of Killekrankie, the white-turreted **Blair Castle** (www.blair-castle.co.uk; Apr–Oct daily 9.30am–5.30pm), seat of the Earls and Dukes of Atholl, is a major tourist destination. The present duke commands Britain's only 'private army', a ceremonial Highland regiment of about 60 local riflemen and 20 pipers and drummers who march in their regalia very occasionally. Part of the castle dates back 700 years, but it has been much reconstructed and restored. It's crammed with possessions amassed by the Atholl family over the centuries: an extensive china collection, swords, rifles, antlers, stuffed animals and portraits. Look in particular for two rare colonial American powder horns, one with a map carved on it that shows forts and settlements around Manhattan Island, Albany, and the Mohawk River.

Further west from Pitlochry is the long and thickly forested **Glen Garry**, one of Scotland's most wonderful mountain valleys. Be sure not to miss the **Falls of Bruar** cascading into the River Garry near the lower end of the glen.

ABERDEEN

The term 'granite city' is self-explanatory when you see the buildings sparkling in the sunshine at **Aberdeen** ⑮. Surprisingly, however, this solid metropolis, further north than Moscow, is anything but sombre: roses, daffodils and crocuses flourish in such profusion that the town has repeatedly won the Britain-in-Bloom trophy.

Scotland's third city is Europe's offshore oil capital, and was one of Britain's major fishing ports. The traditional fishing industry now has a small role to play in the economic life of the city and is mainly reduced to processing fish, while the actual fishing is centred round the port of Peterhead to the north. Most of the boats arriving in the harbour service the great oil rigs and platforms out at sea beyond the horizon. Aberdeen is Scotland's boom city, and its facilities have expanded to accommodate the influx of North Sea oil personnel, creating something of an international atmosphere for the many tourists who visit in the summer.

In the heart of the town, **Marischal College** is the second-largest granite building in the world after the Escorial in Spain. Built of a lighter-coloured variety known as 'white granite', it forms part of the complex of Aberdeen University. The city's first university, King's College, was founded in 1495. Dominating the pleasant quadrangle is the beloved local landmark, the Crown Tower of **King's Chapel**. Knocked down in a storm in 1633, the structure was rebuilt with Renaissance additions. Inside the chapel, look for the arched oak ceiling, carved screen and stalls and Douglas Strachan's modern stained-glass windows.

Marischal Square is the latest area of central Aberdeen to be redeveloped, incorporating some of Aberdeen's historical buildings into a modern setting providing office space, coffee shops and restaurants.

Nearby is the crowded graveyard of the oldest cathedral in Aberdeen, **St Machar's Cathedral**, first built in 1357, and rebuilt in granite in the 15th century. It is the oldest granite

Aberdeen's harbour

building in the city. Capping the marvellous stone interior with its stained-glass windows is a wonderful oak ceiling, bearing seals of kings and religious leaders.

One of Aberdeen's most interesting sites is **Provost Skene's House** (Guestrow, off Broad Street; closed until the completion of the Mari-

Aberdeen, the granite city

schal Square redevelopment), which was built in 1545 is among the oldest houses in Aberdeen. Its rooms span 200 years of period design. In the Painted Gallery is an important cycle of religious art, painted by an unknown 17th-century artist.

The 17th-century **Mercat Cross**, which is ringed by a parapet on which are engraved the names of Scottish monarchs from James I to James VII, is claimed to be the finest example of a burgh (chartered town) cross to survive in Scotland. Aberdeen's charter dates back to 1179.

DUNNOTTAR CASTLE

South of Aberdeen, near Stonehaven, the vast ruins of **Dunnottar Castle** rise above the sea. The fortress has had a rich and varied history. Here, in 1297, William Wallace burned alive an English Plantagenet garrison. Much later, in 1650, the Scottish Crown Regalia were kept here during a siege by Oliver Cromwell's Roundheads. More recently, not to mention more peacefully, the film director Franco Zeffirelli used Dunnottar as the location for his film of *Hamlet*. Note: the steep steps down to the castle may be difficult for less mobile visitors.

Dunnottar Castle

ROYAL DEESIDE

The long, picturesque valley of the River Dee, extending inland from Aberdeen to the high Cairngorm Mountains, has been called **Royal Deeside** since Queen Victoria wrote glowingly about the area. Her 'dear paradise', **Balmoral Castle**, was purchased by Prince Albert in 1852. He refashioned the turreted mansion to his own taste in the Scottish Baronial style; the granite is local, and lighter than Aberdeen's. Balmoral is about 41 miles (66km) west of Aberdeen. If the royal family is not in residence, the grounds are open daily to the public (late Apr–July 10am–5pm; www.balmoralcastle.com). Across the road, modest Crathie Church is attended by the royal family.

Along the Dee near Aberdeen, **Crathes Castle** (www.nts.org.uk; Apr–Oct daily 10.30am–5pm, Nov–Mar Sat–Sun 11am–3.45pm; garden daily 9am–sunset) has some of Scotland's most dramatic gardens, with giant yew hedges that are clipped just once a year. The views from within the 16th-century tower-house over these remarkable hedges are in themselves worth the visit. Look also for the three rooms with painted ceilings, the carved-oak ceiling in the top-floor gallery, and the 14th-century ivory Horn of Leys, above the drawing-room fireplace. The grounds are also home to the Go Ape tree-top adventure.

THE HIGHLANDS

No longer really remote, the sparsely populated north of Scotland offers, above all, superb scenery as well as the country's most mysterious monster and most important distilleries.

THE RIVER SPEY AND THE MALT WHISKY TRAIL

For salmon and whisky, Scotland can offer you nothing better than the **River Spey**. Along this beautiful valley of ferns and old bridges, you'll want to stop to watch anglers casting their long lines into this fastest-flowing river in the British Isles. Nestling among the trees are slate-roofed buildings with pagoda chimneys. Here they produce the finest of all the fine Scotch whiskies, or so the local enthusiasts insist.

The Malt Whisky Trail (www.maltwhiskytrail.com) takes in seven distilleries, which includes one historic distillery and a cooperage, where you can watch malt being distilled by a process that has remained basically unchanged for 500 years. You will usually be invited to enjoy a free wee dram. Contact the local tourist offices to check when the distilleries accommodate visitors and when they're closed. If you're lucky, at the Speyside Cooperage (www.speysidecooperage.co.uk; Mon–Fri 9am–4pm) you'll see a cooper (cask maker) fashioning oak staves into a cask: by law a spirit can't be called 'whisky' until it has been aged in oak for three years. According to the experts, the best maturity for Scotch is about ten years.

Around the malt centre of Dufftown they still like to quote the saying: 'Rome was built on seven hills, Dufftown stands on seven stills' – although at a recent count there were in fact eight distilleries. Some distilleries to visit are **Cardhu Distillery** in Knockando, **Glenfarclas** in Ballinalloch, **Glenfiddich** in Dufftown, **Glen Grant** in Rothes, **Glenlivet** in Glenlivet, and **Strathisla** in Keith.

THE NORTHEAST COAST AND INVERNESS

The northeast coast consists of a fertile coastal plain, shielded to the south by the Cairngorm Mountains. In the 19th century, this area was the centre of a fishing industry, and is dotted with many attractive fishing towns and villages, such as Buckie, Cullen and Portsoy. Just south of Lossiemouth, a fine fishing town and port, lies Elgin, a picturesque town that retains much of its medieval layout, with a cobbled market-place and winding streets. The 13th-century **Elgin Cathedral** was once known as the 'Lantern of the North', and its ruins are still impressive.

In the Highlands, all roads lead to **Inverness ⑯**, capital of the Highlands since the days of the ancient Picts. It is worth stopping in this busy town to tour the small, modern **Museum and Art Gallery** (www.highlifehighland.com; Castle Wynd; Tue–Sat 10am–5pm; free). In a fascinating exhibition

Inverness

of Scottish Highland history dating back to the Stone Age, you can brush up on your clan lore as well as inspect the dirks and sporrans, broadswords, and powder horns.

LOCH NESS

Strategically situated where the River Ness joins the Moray Firth, **Inverness** is not at all shy about exploiting the submarine celebrity presumed to inhabit the waters of **Loch Ness** ⓱ to the south. Nessie T-shirts and all kinds of monster bric-à-brac are on sale. Excursion boats do regular monster-spotting cruises. You can cruise Loch Ness itself, and there are cruises from the Caledonian Canal into Loch Ness. Contact Jacobite Cruises, tel: 01463-233999; www.jacobite.co.uk.

Sonar and underwater cameras have been used by experts to close in on the mystery of the frequent Nessie sightings, and most involved seem to agree that not one, but several large aquatic creatures might roam the very murky depths of Loch Ness, surviving by eating eels and other fish.

Seven rivers feed this loch, bringing in millions of peat particles which reduce visibility to zero below 39ft (12m). At 23 miles (37km) long and about 1 mile (1.5 km) across, Loch Ness is generally about 699ft (213m) deep – though in one area the silted bottom is nearly 1,001ft (305m). That means enough space for a large family of the monster that has intrigued people ever since it was first reported in the 6th century – by no less revered a traveller than St Columba.

Urquhart Castle

Urquhart Castle (daily Apr–Sept 9.30am–6pm, Oct until 5pm, Nov–Mar until 4.30pm) sits by Loch Ness between Fort William and Inverness. Dating back to the 13th century, the castle played a key role in the Wars of Independence, being taken by Edward I and later by Robert the Bruce. Part of the building was blown up in 1692 to prevent it falling into Jacobite hands.

On the busy A82, after leaving the loch, it is virtually impossible to miss the dramatic ruins of **Urquhart Castle** ⑱ (see page 71).

EAST OF INVERNESS

About 5 miles (8km) east of Inverness is **Culloden Battlefield** (www.nts.org.uk; visitor centre daily June–Aug 9am–6pm, Apr–May, Sept 9am–5.30pm, Feb–Mar and Nov–Dec 10am–4pm; site daily year-round), where Bonnie Prince Charlie's Highlanders and the Jacobite cause were defeated by 'Butcher' Cumberland's redcoats in 1746. Jacobite headstones, a visitor centre and exhibition, a 4-minute battle immersion film and a roof-top viewing recall this last major battle fought on British soil. Near the battlefield is the impressive archaeological site of **Clava Cairns**. Three once-domed tombs are encircled by standing stones. To stand in a silent burial chamber dating back to 1800 BC or 1500 BC is a slightly eerie experience.

Between Inverness and Nairn is **Cawdor Castle** (www.cawdorcastle.com; May–early-Oct daily 10am–5pm), a popular site set up to keep the visitor entertained. 'Three out of four Ghosts prefer Cawdor Castle', proclaims the sign at the castle's authentic drawbridge entrance. This fortress home of the Earls of Cawdor is the setting Shakespeare used for the murder of Duncan by Macbeth, although it was actually constructed two centuries after Macbeth's time. The castle has all the features to make it a romantic focus: a drawbridge, an ancient tower and fortified walls. The 1454 tower's Thorn Tree Room is a stone vault enclosing a 600-year-old holly tree. The castle grounds have outstanding flower and kitchen gardens, nature trails, and even a putting green. When you've seen the castle, head for nearby Cawdor village, with its delightful stone cottages set in beautifully tended gardens.

The impressive Clava Cairns

At Carrbridge the **Landmark Forest Adventure Park** (www.landmarkpark.co.uk) provides a wide range of outdoor activities for all the family.

Set against the spectacular backdrop of the Cairngorm Mountains, **Aviemore** ⓳ (see page 92) is one of the most elaborate holiday centres in Scotland, its facilities open all winter for skiing. On a clear day, take a ride up into the mountains on the Cairngorm Mountain Railway. In 2003, the Cairngorms became a National Park, one of only two in Scotland – the other being Loch Lomond and the Trossachs (see page 56).

Some 7 miles (11km) south, the excellent **Highland Wildlife Park** (www.highlandwildlifepark.org.uk; daily Apr–Oct 10am–5pm, July–Aug until 6pm, Nov–Mar 10am–4pm) at Kincraig has a drive-through area (if animals approach, close the windows and remain in your car). You should see the following animals: red deer, yak, musk ox, Przewalski's wild horses, European bison and vicuña. Stars of the walk-through section

Resident tiger, Highland Wildlife Park

include arctic foxes, bears and wildcats. Don't miss the polar bears, two males and a female, who arrived in 2015.

BEN NEVIS AND GLEN COE

The **Great Glen**, which follows the path of a geological fault, makes a scenic drive from Inverness south to Fort William. Near Fort William rises **Ben Nevis**, Great Britain's highest mountain, at 4,406ft (1,344m). More often than not, clouds obscure its rounded summit. The best view of the mountain is from the north, but it is most easily climbed from the west, starting near the bustling Highland touring centre of Fort William. Caution is advised here, as bad weather closes in quickly at the top of Ben Nevis and you can easily get lost.

From Loch Leven, historic **Glen Coe** cuts east through an impressive mountain range. Geology, flora, and fauna are illustrated at a visitor centre (www.nts.org.uk; Apr–Oct daily 9.30am–5.30pm, Nov–Dec Thu–Sun 10am–4pm; site open year-round). In the steep valley, you'll find a memorial to the 1692 massacre of the MacDonalds by the Campbell clan.

From Glen Coe and Fort William, you can take the famed **'Road to the Isles'**, with thoughts of Bonnie Prince Charlie in mind. The route goes past **Neptune's Staircase**, a series of eight lochs, designed by Thomas Telford as part of the Caledonian Canal. The road turns west to **Glenfinnan** (site of a memorial to fallen clansmen at the Battle of Culloden; see page 22) and north along the coast to **Morar**, with its white sandy beaches. One of Scotland's deepest lochs,

Loch Morar, like Loch Ness, has its own monster, Morag. The end of the road is **Mallaig** ⓴, a little town with a picturesque harbour, where the ferry departs for Skye and other Hebridean islands.

THE NORTHWEST COAST

Near Dornie on the road towards Kyle of Lochalsh is the romantic and much-photographed **Eilean Donan Castle** (www.eileandonancastle.com; Apr–Oct daily 10am–6pm, Nov–Dec 10am–4pm, Feb–Mar 10–5pm), connected to the land by a causeway. A Jacobite stronghold, it was destroyed by British warships, but was rebuilt in the 19th century. Today it is a popular tourist destination and has often been used as a film set; *Highlander* was filmed here. It contains a number of Jacobite relics.

A steep hike in the Cairngorms

West from Inverness towards the coast, the dramatic Loch Torridon area is well known for its mountains of red-brown sandstone and white quartzite. These are some of the world's oldest mountains, probably 600 million years old. The **Torridon Countryside Centre** in Torridon (Apr–Sept daily 10am–5pm) offers guided walks in season.

The Gulf Stream works its magic at **Inverewe Garden** ㉑

Subtropical Inverewe Garden

(www.nts.org.uk; gardens daily all year 10am–3pm, extended hours May–Oct, visitor centre June–Aug daily 10am–6pm, May and Sept 10am–5.30pm, Oct 10am–6pm), a subtropical oasis overlooking Loch Ewe, on the same latitude as Juneau, Alaska. The garden was started in 1862 by 20-year-old Osgood Mackenzie on 12,000 acres (4,860 hectares) of barren land, and is one of the world's great plant collections. Late spring and early summer are the best seasons to visit; highlights include giant magnolias and the exotic Himalayan Hound's Tooth.

If you have time for a leisurely tour of Scotland's most spectacular scenery, turn north towards Ullapool. At a fine wooded spot just a minute's walk off the road below Loch Broom are the spectacular Falls of Measach, plunging 200ft (61m) into the **Corrieshalloch Gorge**.

Some of Scotland's most memorable scenery is along the jagged northwest coast above **Ullapool** ㉒, a fishing port and the ferry terminal for the Outer Hebrides. The secondary roads closest to the shore wind through beautiful country filled with mossy rocks, ferns, and hundreds of tiny lochans (small inland lochs). The first section goes through the **Inverpolly National Nature Reserve**. Near Lochinvar, strange stories gather around Suilven, the mount looming over the wild landscape (why don't animals graze on its slopes?). During the summer an excursion boat sets out from tiny

Tarbet to **Handa Island**, a teeming bird sanctuary with huge sandstone cliffs and sandy beaches.

Along Scotland's northern coast near Durness is **Smoo Cave**, which can be found in a beautiful setting at the end of a dramatic sea inlet. The 'gloophole' through the cathedral-like limestone roof of the large outer cavern gets its name from the noise made by air rushing up through it at high tide. Inside the second cave is a 79ft (24m) waterfall. Short boat trips into the cave are available in summer.

A lighthouse stands on **Dunnet Head**, a windy promontory on the northernmost point of the Scottish mainland, over-looking a forbidding sea. If there's no mist, Orkney is visible on the horizon. Nearby **John o'Groats** is far better known, although it isn't quite the most northerly tip of Great Britain. The sign here declares it is 874 miles (1,406km) to Land's End in Cornwall, the greatest overland distance between any two

Ullapool, one of the prettiest villages on the west coast

The Stacks of Duncansby

points in Britain. From John o'Groats, you can take a ferry (May–Sept) to the **Orkney Islands**, which have fascinating archaeological remains – including the Neolithic village of Skara Brae and the Ring of Brodgar.

Offshore from **Duncansby Head**, with its clifftop lighthouse, are the unusual pillar-like Stacks of Duncansby. Inland and to the south, make a short detour from the angling centre of **Lairg** to the Falls of Shin where, with luck, you will see sizeable salmon leaping up low, churning falls along the river.

THE INNER HEBRIDES

MULL

Peaceful moorland glens, sombre mountains, appealing shorelines and one of Scotland's prettiest ports are among the attractions of the large western island of **Mull**. From **Oban 23**, the regular ferry takes 45 minutes to Craignure on Mull, and there is also an 18-minute ferry link between Fishnish Point and Lochaline across the Sound of Mull. In the summer, excursions go from Mull to several smaller islands.

Tobermory 24 (pop. 700), the island's delightful little capital, fits snugly in a harbour ringed by forested hills and protected by flat, green Calve Island. Regattas are held here and golfers enjoy a splendid seascape from the links just above Tobermory. In 1588 a gold-laden galleon from the Spanish

Armada sank here, but salvage efforts ever since have failed. Calgary, to the southwest, which has probably the best of Mull's sandy beaches, inspired the name of the Canadian city about a century ago.

If you're driving and not in a rush, take the coastal road bordering Loch Na Keal. It's slow-going but scenic, along a single track beneath lonely cliffs and hills that are mauve with heather. Dozy sheep get out of your way reluctantly. Gaelic is still spoken here, particularly by the older generation. At the eastern point, visible from the Oban ferry, stand Mull's two castles, both open to the public.

Duart Castle (www.duart castle.com; Apr Sun–Thu 11am–4pm, May–mid–Oct daily 10.30am–5.30pm), on its promontory, guards the Sound of Mull. Dating back to the 12th century, Duart Castle is the home of the chiefs of clan Maclean. The Maclean clan was once a formidable sea power.

An early evening boat trip in Oban

IONA

The sacred island of **Iona** ㉕ lies just off the southwestern tip of Mull. St Columba and about a dozen followers came from Ireland to Iona in 563, bringing to Scotland the culture and learning of the Celtic church, which spread through all of Europe. Some

60 Scottish, Irish, French and Norwegian kings are buried on this sacred island. Centuries of onslaughts by Vikings and others have left no trace of the earliest communities.

Iona is reached via a one-track road and a 10-minute passenger ferry. Iona's 15th-century abbey has been reconstructed and restored. While the ideals of the abbey community cannot be faulted, modernism introduces a jarring note. Other sights are St Martin's Cross, carved in the 10th century; a small Norman chapel, built probably in 1072 by Queen Margaret; the attractive ruins of a 13th-century nunnery; and *Reilig Odhrain*, the graveyard where royalty, Highland chiefs, and more recent islanders are buried. Most of the older stones have been moved inside to preserve them from weather.

On a fine day, take a walk from here to North End where there are beaches of sparkling sand. Most of Iona's inhabitants (around 170) live in the stone houses by the ferry landing. Sheep, cattle and a few fishing boats indicate occupations, but in the summer most islanders are involved with the throngs of visitors and pilgrims that arrive each year. From Iona you can take a boat trip to nearby **Staffa** island, which is home of the dramatic **Fingal's Cave**, a natural wonder which inspired part of Mendelssohn's *Hebrides Overture*. You can also get to Staffa from Mull or Oban.

SKYE

This best-loved Highland island is outrageously beautiful – whether the sun is shining or mists are swirling around its startling hills and idyllic glens. **Skye** is a 5-minute ferry trip from Kyle of Lochalsh, or 30 minutes from Mallaig. The Skye Bridge (toll free) links Kyleakin on Skye with Kyle of Lochalsh. **Portree** ㉖, with its colourful harbour, is the island's main town. Together with **Broadford**, these are the most popular centres for touring, but the island has many quieter places to stay.

The interesting **Clan Donald Centre** and the beautiful **Armadale Castle Gardens** ㉗ (www.clandonald.com; daily Apr–Oct 9.30am–5.30pm) are 16 miles (25km) south of Broadford, near the ferry terminal from Mallaig. For centuries the Macdonalds had styled themselves 'Lords of the Isles' and the Museum of the Isles has an exhibit detailing the history of the Highlands. The gardens and nature walks are outstanding.

St Martin's Cross on Iona

Two remarkable ranges of peaks, the Black Cuillins in the south and the Quiraing in the north, make the island a hiker's or rock-climber's paradise (see page 91). Inside the wild and jagged **Cuillin Hills** is Loch Coruisk, which can be reached by boat from Elgol. Isolated by high peaks all around, the blue-black water of Coruisk has an eerie beauty. The hamlets of Ord and Tarskavaig are worth visiting on a clear day for their splendid views of the Cuillins.

Dunvegan Castle ㉘ (www.dunvegancastle.com; Apr–mid-Oct daily 10am–5pm, mid-Oct–Mar group appointments only), northwest of Portree, has been the stronghold of the chiefs of MacLeod for more than seven centuries and is still the home of the chief of the clan. On display within this sturdy loch-side fortress is the Fairy Flag, a fragile remnant of silk believed to have been woven in Rhodes during the 7th century. Supposedly it saved the MacLeods in clan battles twice, and still has the power to do so one more time. Rather more down-to-earth is a pit dungeon – 13ft (4m) deep – into which prisoners were lowered from an upstairs chamber, though the grim aspect of the dungeon is somewhat diluted by a 'prisoner' and an audio of his groans. Samuel Johnson and James Boswell were

Cuillin Hills viewed from Kyle of Lochalsh

entertained here in 1773, and supplied with fresh horses to continue their journey.

From Dunvegan pier small boats make frequent half-hour trips to offshore rocks and islets to get close to the seals. The seals also appear, though less regularly, all around Skye's 998 miles (1,609km) of coastline.

Old Man of Storr

The dramatic collection of rocks known as the **Quiraing**, accessed more easily than the Cuillins, dominates the landscape north of the secondary road between Staffin and Uig, the ferry port for the Outer Hebrides. Reached by foot, the various rock features here include the castellated crags of the Prison, the slender 100ft (30m) Needle and the Table, a meadow as large as a football field.

Far north at Kilmuir are the grave and monument to Skye's romantic heroine, **Flora MacDonald**, who smuggled fugitive Bonnie Prince Charlie, disguised as her female servant, to safety. On the picturesque coast of Staffin, the Kilt Rock is a curiously fluted cliff with a waterfall that plunges down to the sea. Be extremely careful on this lofty ridge.

A mile futher on, the Lealt Falls tumble down a long and accessible ravine into the sea at a pretty little cove. Salmon can sometimes be seen leaping here. Closer to Portree you will see a giant rock pinnacle called **Old Man of Storr**; there is a forest walk in the vicinity.

WHAT TO DO

Wherever you might be staying in Scotland, particularly from spring to autumn, there's plenty to do. There's a range of information on the VisitScotland website (www.visitscotland.com) and you can download brochures. The outdoors always beckons and you'll come across many local happenings as you travel around.

ENTERTAINMENT

Most newsagents in Glasgow and Edinburgh stock *The List* (www.list.co.uk), a guide to events, theatre, cinema and clubs in both cities and their surrounding areas, which is published every two months.

SPECIAL EVENTS

Highland Games are staged all over the country during the summer months. In addition to kilted titans tossing a huge pine trunk – the famous caber – there'll be pipe and drum bands and accomplished shows of Highland dancing. The most famous of these events is the **Braemar Highland Gathering**, in early September, often attended by members of the royal family and the queen herself, a custom started by Queen Victoria. Also of interest are the agricultural shows and sheepdog trials held in a number of farming areas.

Throughout the summer there are country fairs and many re-enactments of battles and other historic events. In July, the **Scottish Transport Extravaganza** at Glamis Castle, an exhibition of vintage vehicles, is the largest event of its kind in Scotland. **Ceilidhs**, or **folk nights**, which are held frequently in all parts of Scotland, feature dancers, pipers, fiddlers and a range of other artists. Folk festivals are staged in centres from Edinburgh to Stornaway. There has been a revival of Gaelic

Throwing the hammer at the Perth Highland Games

music and both the traditional and the modern-style music performed by groups like Capercaillie, Breabach and Salsa Celtica are enormously popular.

Of course, the most significant special event is the **Edinburgh International Festival**, which takes place in August. Virtuoso performances of music, opera, dance, and theatre are staged by artists of international reputation. Tickets are in great demand so book early both for tickets and hotel rooms. The **Edinburgh Festival Fringe** is less predictable but increasingly popular and often highly innovative. Other cultural high spots include Glasgow's **West End Festival** and the **Perth Arts Festival**.

Performing on the Royal Mile during the Edinburgh Festival

MUSIC AND THEATRE

The redeveloped Theatre Royal in Glasgow is home to the **Scottish Opera**. The Glasgow Royal Concert Hall is the main venue for classical music, with regular concerts by the **Royal Scottish National Orchestra**. Both also perform regularly in Edinburgh, home to the prestigious Scottish Chamber Orchestra. The churches in both cities regularly host excellent concerts. The prestigious BBC Scottish Symphony Orchestra is based at City Halls in Glasgow, taking live music across the country.

Both cities have first-rate **theatre** scenes, with high-quality productions all year round. The Citizens' Theatre in Glasgow presents serious drama, with more avant-garde shows at the Tramway and the Tron. In Edinburgh,

Festival fever

Also held during the Edinburgh Festival are the Military Tattoo, Book Festival, Film Festival and the Jazz and Blues Festival. For details visit www.edinburghcity.com.

the Traverse launches experimental work and the Royal Lyceum mounts a classical repertory. Shows, musicals and touring companies are also on the agenda. An important theatre season takes place over the summer in **Pitlochry** (see page 63). Other centres for regional theatre are St Andrews, Banchory, and Tobermory on Mull. Stirling's Tolbooth is a centre for the arts and music, and a Robert Burns festival takes place in Dumfries.

Major **rock bands** appear at Hampden Park in Glasgow or occasionally Murrayfield Stadium in Edinburgh. Other main venues in Glasgow are the SECC and the Barrowland Ballroom. The **Glasgow International Jazz Festival** in June brings in jazz musicians from all over the world.

CLUBS AND PUBS

Pubs are very popular with the locals everywhere in Scotland and are especially crowded around the end of the working day and at weekends. The scene is lively and while the drinking man's bar still exists, most pubs now have a relaxed and friendly atmosphere. Thanks to changes in Scottish licensing laws, even children are welcome in many pubs. An increasing number serve good food. Many pubs in the cities also offer live music in the evening. Some pubs, especially in Edinburgh, have their own resident folk or jazz musicians. In Glasgow, you can choose between traditional pubs and upmarket, fashionable bars. Café-bars are plentiful in Edinburgh.

Fly fishing

SPORT AND RECREATION

Scotland's outdoors attracts more visitors than its castles, museums or even the Edinburgh Festival.

FISHING

Scotland's rivers, lochs and coastal waters offer some of the finest game fishing in Europe. Much of it is free or very cheap; you don't need a general fishing licence, just a local permit. However, casting your line in the highly prized salmon beats costs hundreds of pounds per week, and you may have to book a year ahead for the privilege.

The **Spey**, **Tay** and **Tweed** are famous for salmon, sea trout and brown trout, though these fish also run in other Scottish waters. Most angling is fly; occasionally spinner or bait is permitted. If you'd like to learn the difference between a dry fly and an insect or how to stay upright while wading and casting in a rushing burn, experts are on hand all over Scotland. The VisitScotland website (www.visitscotland.com) and www.fish pal.com have information on fishing, with details of the best places, seasons and necessary permits. Fishing for salmon and sea trout is not allowed on Sundays and it is illegal for anglers to sell rod-caught salmon. Coarse fishing for perch and pike is permitted year-round, including Sundays, and can be very good, particularly in southern waters.

Sea-angling trips run from ports along the Scottish coast and the islands; or you can fish from countless perches on the shoreline. Some species of fish, such as dogfish and mackerel, can be found in abundance, and towards the end of the summer you might well hook blue or porbeagle shark.

For more information, contact the **Scottish Anglers National Association** (National Game Angling Centre, The Pier, Loch Leven, Kinross; tel: 01577-861116; www.sana.org.uk).

GOLF

Scotland is the original home of golf, a powerful lure for visitors wanting to play on the famous links. Many of Scotland's courses are municipal courses open to everyone. To play the famous courses, it helps to have a letter from your golf club at home stating your experience and handicap. If you choose your hotels or a special golfing-holiday package with care, you can play a different course each day for a week. The Scots make a distinction between two types of courses: links courses are on or near the sea; parkland (or heathland) courses are inland, often on hilly terrain.

St Andrews, home of the **Royal and Ancient Golf Club** has seven courses of its own, with a further 45 across Fife. Visitors with an ambition to play the historic **Old Course**

LINKS LINEAGE

When exactly golf began along the sandy coast in this chilly and windy land isn't clear, but the earliest record dates from 1457, when James II tried to outlaw golf as a menace to national security – too many Scots marksmen were skipping archery practice to swing at the little ball. Mary, Queen of Scots loved the game so much that she risked criticism by taking to the fairways while in mourning for her murdered husband. She is thought to have played at Bruntsfield in Edinburgh, probably the oldest course on which golf is still played today.

should apply in writing to the St Andrews Links Trust (www.
standrews.com) in August/September for the following year
for a pre-booked tee-time, or enter the daily 'ballot', a lot-
tery to determine which lucky applicants will fill vacancies
and cancellations the following day. You can book any of the
St Andrews courses at the **Club**, tel: 01334-466666. Other
outstanding Scottish golf courses include **Carnoustie**, **Royal
Troon**, **Gleneagles**, **Muirfield**, **Royal Dornoch** and **Turnberry.**

BIKING, HIKING AND MOUNTAIN-CLIMBING

Biking. For more information about bicycling in Scotland see
the VisitScotland website: www.visitscotland.com/see-do/
activities. The rolling hills of
Fife are especially good for
cycling and there is a 300-
mile (500km) sign posted
cycle network. See www.
outdoorfife.com for details.

Biking in the Cairngorms

Hiking. Scotland's beautiful landscape offers unrivalled opportunities for
hiking and hill walking. The
West Highland Way begins in
Milngavie north of Glasgow
and continues on past Loch
Lomond up to Fort William.
The Southern Upland Way and
Speyside Way are also popular
for long-distance walks. There
are also many guided walks.
In the Highlands, particularly,
you will find nature walks and
hill or plateau excursions

led by trained naturalists. Week-long hikes over moors and glens include meals and accommodation in the price. At **Glen Coe** and **Torridon** the National Trust for Scotland conducts several superb guided walks. VisitScotland (www.visitscotland.com/see-do/activities) has a range of walks on its website.

Mountain-climbing. You can take a strenuous walk up

Climbing caveats

Despite a concentrated campaign for safety, mountain climbers continue to get into trouble in Scotland. Always get local advice on weather and conditions. Weather can change rapidly and suddenly, especially in the Highlands. Be sure you take the proper equipment and let someone know where you are going. Never go alone.

Britain's highest mountain, **Ben Nevis** (see page 74), climb the peaked ridges of the Isle of **Arran** (see page 47) or go rock climbing in the Black Cuillins, depending on your skills. While their height is not great, the remote **Cuillins** on Skye offer some of the most challenging climbing in Britain (see page 81). The **Mountaineering Council of Scotland** in Perth (www.mcofs.org.uk; tel: 01738-493942) can provide maps and telephone numbers to call for advice.

BOATING AND WATERSPORTS

Depending on your expertise, you can hire any sort of boat to explore Scotland's marvellous inland and coastal waters. **Sailing** schools offer courses for beginners all along Scotland's coast. If you have documentation to prove your proficiency, you may be able to charter larger craft without a skipper.

Water-skiing is popular on the placid waters of Scotland's lochs. **Windsurfing** is available at all levels inland, on lochs, or on the open sea. Summer days can be surprisingly hot, and swimming opportunities are abundant. Be alert, however, for dangerous undertows and rip currents off western coasts.

The transparency of Scotland's waters makes them ideal for **scuba diving**. There are sub-aqua sites all around the coast, in various inland lochs and on the islands.

For further information on watersports in Scotland, see Visit-Scotland's website (www.visitscotland.com/see-do/activities).

PONY TREKKING AND RIDING

All over Scotland there are horse and pony centres where you can ride by the hour, half day or full day. Pony treks are led by expert guides and some are suitable for young children. Horseback trail riding is only for experienced riders. Some centres offer accommodation and weekly programmes with a different excursion each day. See the VisitScotland website (www.visitscotland.com/see-do/activities) for a list of reputable riding stables.

SKIING

Scotland has five major downhill ski centres: **Cairngorm** in Inverness-shire, **Glen Coe Mountain Resort** in Glen Coe, the **Nevis mountain range** in Inverness-shire, the **Lecht** and **Glenshee**, both in Aberdeenshire. The Cairngorms are Britain's highest mountains, and **Aviemore**, its centre, has buses to the ski areas, which have runs for skiers of all abilities. You'll find instructors, chairlifts, equipment hire, tows and accommodation at all the main ski areas; there's also the Cairngorm Mountain Railway. The ski season is December to May, though snowfall can be

Football is hugely popular

unpredictable (for updates: http://ski.visitscotland.com).

SPECTATOR SPORTS

Rugby and football are as popular in Scotland as in the rest of the UK. Glasgow's Celtic and Rangers are the most successful soccer teams. International competitions take place in Hampden Park Stadium. You may also want to observe the Scottish game of curling, a bit like bowling on ice, which has been practised in Scotland for at least 400 years.

Glasgow's Princes Square

SHOPPING

Shops are generally open 9am–5.30pm Monday to Saturday (a few places may close on Saturday afternoon), and major shopping centres in cities are also open on Sunday. In the Highlands, however, Sunday closing is the rule. In smaller towns, check whether there is an early closing day.

Glasgow is Scotland's major shopping city. Main areas are the smart, upmarket **Princes Square**, the newly developed Buchanan Quarter and Ingram Street, known as Glasgow's style mile. Also popular is the St Enoch Centre, the largest glass structure in Europe. In Edinburgh the main shopping is on **Princes Street**, with fashion chains, bookshops and department stores. For gifts, tartans and other Scottish wares, there are plenty of shops on the **Royal Mile**. For upmarket shopping, visit Multrees Walk just off St Andrew

Square, centred around the Harvey Nichols store, and for vintage and boutique shops check out Stockbridge.

Value Added Tax (VAT). Almost all merchandise and services are subject to 20 percent Value Added Tax (VAT). For major purchases over a certain amount of money, overseas visitors can get a VAT refund. Note that this applies only to shops that are members of the Retail Export Scheme. When you make your purchase, request a signed form and a stamped pre-addressed envelope; have your form stamped by British Customs as you leave the country and post the form back to the shop to obtain a refund. You can also avoid the VAT if you do your shopping in duty-free shops – look for the sign.

Edinburgh's Grassmarket

Visitors from EU countries should present the form to their home customs, who will insert the local VAT rate for the goods. This form should also be posted back to the shop for a refund.

WHAT TO BUY

Art and Antiques. The Scottish art scene is an active one. Look for prints and affordable works by young Scottish artists. Victorian antiques and old prints and maps are also a good buy.

Crafts. In the Highlands you will find interesting stoneware and salt-glazed pottery. There are potters, jewellery makers and other craftspeople on the Isles of Mull and Skye. Unusual 'heathergems' jewellery is made from stems of heather. Look out for wood and stag-horn carvings, Celtic designs, handknits and hand-made greetings cards.

Crystal. A number of high-quality glass and crystal producers have come from Scotland, including Caithness Glass, Selkirk Glass, Edinburgh Crystal and Stuart Crystal. There's also the

Dog and whisky in Edinburgh

Caithness Glass visitor centre in Crieff (www.caithnessglass.co.uk), where you can buy beautiful paperweights.

Kilts and Tartans. A number of shops in Edinburgh, Glasgow, Stirling and Aberdeen specialise in made-to-measure kilts, or full Highland dress. These shops will be glad to help you find your family tartan.

Knitwear and Woollens. Scottish knitwear includes cashmere pullovers and cardigans and Shetland and Fair Isle sweaters. Tartan woollens can be bought by the yard, and you can see them woven at several woollen mills. Harris tweed and sheepskin rugs are also popular buys.

Jewellery. In Glasgow (and elsewhere), look for sterling and enamel jewellery made from the designs of Charles Rennie Mackintosh. Silvercraft from Orkney and Shetland has designs inspired by Norse mythology. Celtic-designed jewellery, clan brooches and ornate kilt pins are often produced in pewter. And for the romantics there's the delicately worked luckenbooth, a traditional Scottish love token.

Whisky. Scotch whisky is not necessarily less expensive in Scotland, but you'll find brands that you never knew existed, so take the opportunity to discover an unusual malt.

CHILDREN'S ACTIVITIES

VisitScotland's website (www.visitscotland.com/see-do/family) gives information on where to take the kids. Children enjoy exploring Scottish castles and there are many country parks with farm animals and playgrounds. Highland Games offer colourful spectacles with plenty of side shows (see page 85).

In Edinburgh, children will enjoy the Museum of Childhood on the Royal Mile (see page 34) and the National Museum of Scotland (see page 33). Older children will like the scary thrills of the **Edinburgh Dungeon**, (www.thedungeons.com; 31 Market Street, next to Waverley Bridge; daily 10am–5pm, mid-July–Aug until 7pm). Both children and adults will find Our Dynamic Earth (see page 36) fascinating. **Edinburgh Zoo**, 3 miles (5km) from the centre, is Scotland's largest, on 80 acres (32 hectares) of hillside parkland (134 Corstorphine Road; tel: 0131-334 9171; www.edinburghzoo.org.uk; daily Mar and Oct 9am–5pm, Apr–Sept until 6pm, Nov–Feb 9am–4.30pm; penguin parade daily at 2.15pm, but only if the penguins feel like it).

At Coatbridge on the M8 motorway near Glasgow, the **Time Capsule** (www.thetimecapsule.info) offers fun for all with water chutes, ice skating and a soft play area.

Star-gazing at the National Museum of Scotland

CALENDAR OF EVENTS

January Celtic Connections, traditional music festival, www.celtic connections.com, Glasgow. 25 January: Burns Night, Scotland-wide. Last Tuesday in January: Up Helly Aa, fire festival, Lerwick, Shetland.

February Fort William Mountain Film Festival, for outdoor enthusiasts, www.mountainfilmfestival.co.uk.

March Glasgow International Comedy Festival, www.glasgowcomedy festival.com. Easter ski events, www.ski-scotland.com.

April Edinburgh International Harp Festival, www.harpfestival.co.uk. Scottish Grand National, Ayr, www.ayr-racecourse.co.uk.

Late April–May Spirit of Speyside Whisky Festival, www.spiritofspeyside.com. Perth Festival of the Arts, www.perthfestival.co.uk.

June Common Ridings, festival of marking town boundaries on horseback, Scottish Borders. West End Festival, including the Festival Sunday Parade, Glasgow, www.westendfestival.co.uk. Royal Highland Show, farming event, Ingliston, near Edinburgh, www.royalhighland show.org. Edinburgh International Film Festival, www.edfilmfest.org. uk. Glasgow International Jazz Festival.

July Scottish Traditional Boat Festival, Portsoy, Aberdeenshire, www. stbfportsoy.com. Aberdeen Asset Management Scottish Open, golf tournament, www.aamscottishopen.com. The Wickerman Festival, alternative music festival, East Kirkcarswell, Dumfries & Galloway, www.thewickermanfestival.co.uk. Edinburgh Jazz and Blues Festival.

August Edinburgh International Festival, www.eif.co.uk. Edinburgh Fringe Festival, www.edfringe.com. Edinburgh Military Tattoo, www. edintattoo.co,uk. World Pipe Band Championship, Glasgow.

September First Saturday: Braemar Highland Gathering, www. braemargathering.org. Doors Open Days, visit the country's best architecture for free, Scotland-wide, www.doorsopendays.org.uk.

October Royal National Mod, Gaelic festival, various locations.

November 30 November (and week running up to it), St Andrew's Day, St Andrews and Scotland-wide.

December 31 December: Hogmanay, Scotland-wide. Stonehaven Fireball Festival, traditional parade, www.stonehavenfireballs.co.uk.

EATING OUT

The Scots are very proud of the amount of good cooking to be found throughout their country, even in the remotest spots. Scottish chefs have won many accolades at international culinary competitions, and the better hotels and country house hotels may be staffed by award-winning chefs. The tourist office's 'Taste of Scotland' initiative has encouraged chefs to rethink traditional dishes, using the freshest local ingredients. Chefs make full use of these local basics: fresh salmon and trout, herring, beef, venison, grouse, pheasant, potatoes, raspberries, and other fruit and vegetables. Oatmeal turns up in all kinds of dishes. Long gone are the days of Samuel Johnson's oft-quoted remark about oats after he toured the northern regions of Scotland: '...a grain which in England is generally given to horses, but in Scotland supports the people'.

A full Scottish breakfast

Much Scottish fare is hearty, intended to act as a fortification against the weather. Whenever possible, try traditional dishes, which are often delicious. Vegetarian options are widely available in the cities, and are increasingly offered in smaller towns and villages.

WHEN TO EAT

Outside the cities, restaurants, roadside inns and
snack bars are rather thin
on the ground. Even in the
cities, many of the finest
Scottish restaurants are in
hotels; non-residents are
usually welcome, but check

Further info

The List's Eating and Drinking Guide provides listings
for Edinburgh and Glasgow;
www.list.co.uk. For restaurants serving traditional
Scottish food visit www.taste-
of-scotland.com.

with guest houses or smaller establishments. In the summer, it is a good idea to book ahead, particularly if the
restaurant is known for its fine cuisine. If you are touring,
picnic lunches are a good idea – you may find yourself miles
from any food outlets and there is certainly no shortage of
lovely sites.

Breakfast, usually from around 8am–10am, is provided by
practically every hotel and guest house in Scotland. Away
from major centres, restaurants may not serve lunch before
noon or much after 2pm, and dinner may only be served
between 7 and 9pm.

In general, restaurant prices compare favourably with
those south of the border. This does not prevent certain
Scottish establishments from charging prices that would
not be out of place in London's West End. Keep in mind
the inclusion in restaurant prices of 20 percent VAT sales
tax, and often a 10 percent service charge. A full Scottish
breakfast is usually included in your hotel or bed and
breakfast tariff.

While a light lunch at midday and more substantial dinner
in the evening may be the style in tourist areas, conversely,
in the countryside dinner is sometimes what the substantial
midday meal is called, while the lighter evening meal may be
called tea or supper.

Try Arbroath smokies while in Scotland

WHAT TO EAT

BREAKFAST

Unlike England, where some hotels have converted to the 'continental breakfast', the Scottish breakfast still gives you the works. Porridge is served with cream or milk (and sugar, though this is frowned upon by traditionalists, who prefer salt and use water instead of milk), followed by fruit juice, fresh fruit, eggs, sausage, bacon, tomatoes, mushrooms, potato scones, rolls, jam and marmalade. A special touch is the addition of the Scottish kipper and smoked haddock – it's hard to argue with the conventional wisdom that Loch Fyne kippers are best, but it is equally hard to find a smoked herring from anywhere in Scotland that isn't delicious. The famous Arbroath smokies are salted haddock flavoured with hot birch or oak smoke. Finnan haddock (or haddie) are salted and smoked over peat. Pâtés of kipper, trout, smoked salmon and haddock have become favourite starters in good restaurants.

MAIN COURSES

Fish and Shellfish. Scottish smoked salmon is famous all over the world, thanks to the special flavours introduced by the distinctive peat or oak-chip smoking process. Farmed salmon is now widely available, and while the purist may argue that it isn't as good as the wild variety, there are few people who can actually tell the difference.

Nothing is better than a whole fresh salmon poached with wine and vegetables. The west coast is renowned for the excellence of its lobster, scallops, crayfish, mussels and oysters.

Meat and Game. Scottish beef rivals the best in Europe. Aberdeen Angus steak is a favourite, served with a mushroom-and-wine sauce. Whisky goes into many sauces served with beef: Gaelic steak, for instance, is seasoned with garlic and fried with sautéed onions, with whisky added during the cooking process. Whisky is also used in preparing seafood,

SCOTCH BROTH

Traditional Scottish soups are best if they are homemade. Try a few of the following:

Cock-a-leekie – a seasoned broth made from boiling fowl with leeks and at times onions and prunes. Consumed for at least 400 years and dubbed the national soup of Scotland.

Partan bree – creamed crab (partan) soup.

Scotch broth – a variety of vegetables in a barley-thickened soup with mutton or beef.

Cullen skink – milky broth of Finnan haddock with onions and potatoes.

Lorraine – a creamy chicken soup made with nutmeg, almonds and lemon, named after Mary of Guise-Lorraine.

Oatmeal – made with onion, leek, carrot and turnip.

poultry and game. *Forfar bridies* are pastry puffs stuffed with minced steak and onions. If you are lucky, you might also find beef collops (slices) in pickled walnut sauce. Veal is rather scarce. In recent years, lamb has appeared more frequently, sometimes in ingenious dishes.

Game still abounds in Scotland. After the shooting season opens (on the 'glorious 12th' of August), grouse is an expensive but much sought-after dish, served in a pie or roasted with crispy bacon and served with bread sauce or fried breadcrumbs. Venison appears frequently on the menu, often roasted or in a casserole. You will also find pheasant, guinea fowl, quail and hare in terrines, pâtés and game pies.

Haggis and whisky

Haggis. Haggis, Scotland's national dish, hardly deserves its horrific reputation among non-Scots. Properly made, it consists of chopped-up sheep's innards, oatmeal, onions, beef suet and seasoning, boiled in a sewn-up sheep's stomach bag. Haggis is traditionally accompanied by *chappit tatties* and *bashed neeps* – mashed potatoes and turnips.

Other traditional dishes are *Scotch eggs*: hard-boiled eggs coated with sausage meat and breadcrumbs, deep-fried and eaten hot or cold. *Scotch woodcock* is toast topped with anchovy and scrambled egg.

Potatoes and Oatmeal. Potatoes are a particular local pride. *Stovies* are leftovers from the Sunday roast, usually including potatoes, onions, carrots, gravy and occasionally the meat, cooked in the dripping. *Rumbledethumps* are

> ### Skirlie
>
> *Skirlie* is a mixture of oatmeal and onions flavoured with thyme. Oatmeal also turns up as a coating on such foods as herring and cheese and in desserts.

a mixture of boiled cabbage and mashed potatoes (sometimes onions or chives and grated cheese are added). You should not have to go all the way to northernmost Caithness for Scotland's basic dish of *tatties* (potatoes boiled in their skin) and herrings. And in the Orkney Islands they like *clapshot* (potatoes and turnips mashed together and seasoned with fresh black pepper) to accompany their haggis.

AFTERNOON TEA, DESSERT AND CHEESE

Tea rooms all over Scotland offer afternoon tea, with sandwiches, cakes and other delicacies. Shortbread is, of course, a Scottish speciality. Another classic Scottish speciality is rich, dark Dundee cake, made with dried fruits and spices and topped with almonds. Dundee also contributed bitter orange marmalade to the world in the 1700s. Scones and bannocks (oatmeal cakes) are among the great array of Scottish baked and griddled goods. A teatime treat is Scotch pancakes, served with butter and marmalade or honey. Oatcakes come either rough or smooth and they are eaten on their own or with butter, pâté, jam, or crowdie, Scotland's centuries-old version of cottage cheese. In Edinburgh, the afternoon tea at the Balmoral Hotel is famous, and in Glasgow, don't miss going to one of the Willow Tea Rooms, designed by Charles Rennie Mackintosh.

For dessert, you'll see various combinations of cheese, with red berries or black cherries and vanilla ice cream.

Glenmorangie distillery

Cranachan, a tasty Scottish speciality, consists of toasted oatmeal and cream and whisky or rum topped with nuts and raspberries or other soft fruit. Rhubarb-and-ginger tart is worth looking out for, as is butterscotch tart.

Scotland produces several excellent varieties of cheddar cheese and recent years have seen a rediscovery of old Scottish cheeses. Produced (although on a small scale) throughout the country, the speciality cheeses are characterised by a high degree of individuality. Try Criffel, Lanark blue, Isle of Mull or creamy Crannog or Orkney Cheddar.

WHAT TO DRINK

A huge amount of folklore surrounds every aspect of **Scotch whisky,** from its distillation using pure mountain water, to the aroma of the peat, to its storage, all the way to the actual drinking. The word 'whisky' derives from the Gaelic *uisge beatha* 'water of life'. It is available in two basic types – *malt* (distilled solely from malted barley) and *grain* (made from malted barley and grain). Most of the Scotch sold today is blended, combining malt and grain whiskies. There are now more than 2,000 brands of authentic Scotch whisky.

The malt whiskies come primarily from Speyside and the Highlands, and each has its own distinctive flavour: dry, smoky, peppery, peaty or sweet. Purists insist that a single-malt whisky should be drunk only neat or with plain water – never with other mixers, although these are acceptable with blended Scotch, even by Scots.

After dinner, Scotland's version of Irish coffee, which naturally uses local whisky, may be called a 'Gaelic coffee'. A rusty nail, believed for obvious reasons to have associations with a coffin nail, is one measure of malt whisky plus one measure of Drambuie. A 'Scotch mist' is made from whisky, squeezed lemon rind and crushed ice, shaken well. An 'Atholl Brose' blends oatmeal, heather honey and whisky.

Because of the country's long-standing association with France – the 'Auld Alliance' against the English – good French **wine**, especially claret, was on Scottish tables before it was widely available in England. Most reputable hotels and restaurants offer an extensive wine list, often now including good wines from New Zealand, Australia and Chile.

Scotland is proud of its **beer**. The Scottish equivalent of English 'bitter' is called 'heavy', and should be served at room temperature. The 'half and a half' featured in old-fashioned pubs is a dram of whisky with a half pint of beer as a chaser.

Whisky in Glen Coe

PLACES TO EAT

*We have used the following symbols to give an idea of the price
for a 3-course meal for one person without wine or service.*

££££ over £45   **££** £22–£32
£££ £32–£45   **£** under £22

EDINBURGH AND LOTHIAN

Champany Inn £££ *Champany, Linlithgow, West Lothian, tel: 01506-834532*, www.champany.com. Open Monday–Friday for lunch and dinner, Saturday dinner only. Acclaimed for its steaks and wine cellar, and set in an old mill with beamed ceilings and antique tables. An informal, moderately priced 'Chop and Ale House' adjoins. Reservations advised.

Contini Ristorante ££ *103 George Street, tel: 0131-225 1550*, www.contini.com. Open daily for breakfast, lunch and dinner. The name may have changed at Centotre, as it was formerly known, but the same family still serve the same delicious northern Italian food.

Gusto ££ *135 George Street, tel: 0131-225 2555*, www.gusto restaurants.uk.com. Open daily for lunch and dinner. A typical trattoria with a modern twist: open-kitchen, stainless-steel decor, and a bustling atmosphere combined with traditional Italian cooking.

Henderson's of Edinburgh £ *94 Hanover Street, tel: 0131-225 2131*, www.hendersonsofedinburgh.co.uk. Open Monday–Saturday for breakfast, lunch and dinner; bistro and deli open Sunday. Eat in the basement restaurant, upstairs in the bistro or take something home from the deli. Perfect for vegetarians, it offers salads, vegetarian pasta and moussaka, or vegetarian haggis with neeps and tatties. Good desserts, organic wines, plus live music in the evening.

The Honours £££ *58a North Castle Street, tel: 0131-220 2513*, www.thehonours.co.uk. Open Tuesday–Saturday for lunch and dinner. From the Martin Wishart stable, this option in New Town is to his same high standards and boasts a brasserie-style French menu.

Howies ££ *29 Waterloo Place, tel: 0131-556 5766*, www.howies. uk.com. Open daily for lunch and dinner. Elegant Georgian setting to enjoy Scottish and French cuisine consisting of fresh, tasty ingredients in an informal atmosphere. Also open from 11am for coffee.

Number One ££££ *The Balmoral Hotel, 1 Princes Street tel: 0131-557 6727*, www.restaurantnumberone.com. Open daily for lunch and dinner. World-class cooking, using the best of Scottish produce, at this wonderfully stylish Michelin-starred restaurant.

Pickles £ *56a Broughton Street, tel: 0131-557 5005*, www.get pickled.co.uk. Open daily 4.30pm–late. For something different and a little lighter, this chill-out place offers delicious platters featuring Scottish cheeses or meat and, naturally, a huge range of pickles and sides.

Timberyard £££ *10 Lady Lawson Street, tel: 0131-221 1222*, www. timberyard.co. Open Tuesday–Sunday for lunch and dinner. Located in a former warehouse, this family business is about respecting the environment. Only local artisans' ingredients go into the imaginative dishes, and some produce is grown on-site.

VinCaffè ££ *11 Multrees Walk, tel: 0131-557 0088*, www.valvona crolla.co.uk. Open daily for coffee, lunch and dinner. Part of the legendary Italian family institution, Valvona and Crolla, so well-loved throughout the city. The upstairs wine bar is relaxed yet sophisticated, serving excellent pastas and antipasto to complement the wine list, and downstairs there's an Italian café.

The Witchery by the Castle ££££ *352 Castlehill, Royal Mile, tel: 0131-225 5613*, www.thewitchery.com. Open daily for lunch and dinner. Whether it is Aberdeen Angus beef or Scottish lobster the cooking at the Witchery won't disappoint and a galaxy of celebrities would agree. Good pre-theatre suppers help to keep the cost down.

SOUTH AND BORDERS

Carrick Lodge ££ *46 Carrick Road, Ayr, tel: 01292-262 846*, www.carricklodgehotel.co.uk. Open daily for lunch and dinner. This hotel restaurant delivers great service along with a mouth-watering combination of flavours. Pigeon breast with black pudding is a popular starter, as is hoi sin, ginger and chilli-caramelised salmon for mains.

Kailzie Gardens Restaurant £ *Near Peebles (on the B7062), tel: 01721-722807*, www.kailziegardens.com. Open Wednesday–Sunday for brunch, lunch and tea. This delightful restaurant serves wholesome home-cooked lunches and fine afternoon teas inspired by local suppliers.

Marmions Brasserie ££ *Buccleuch Street, Melrose, the Borders, tel: 01896-822245*, www.marmionsbrasserie.co.uk. Open Monday–Saturday for breakfast, lunch and dinner. Relaxed, friendly restaurant with good use of local produce. A good place to stop for lunch when touring the Border abbeys.

Simply Scottish £ *6–8 High Street, Jedburgh, Roxburghshire, tel: 01835-864696*. Open daily for coffee and lunch. A café that serves sophisticated and contemporary Scottish fare, made from the freshest ingredients.

GLASGOW

Babbity Bowster £ *16–18 Blackfriars Street, tel: 0141-552 5055*, www.babbitybowster.com. Open daily for lunch and dinner. The popular downstairs café-bar serves seafood and Scottish fare with a French influence, but for a quieter, more intimate dinner, it's advisable to eat upstairs in the charming dining room (dinner only Tuesday–Saturday). You can stay here too, but it can sometimes be very noisy.

Café Gandolfi £ *64 Albion St, tel: 0141-552 6813*, www.cafegandolfi.com. Open daily for morning coffee, lunch, tea and dinner. In the heart of Glasgow's merchant city, this restaurant offers good, simple food in a pleasant atmosphere.

Drum and Monkey £ *91 St Vincent Street, tel: 0141-221* 6636. This casual pub-restaurant serves Scottish-French cuisine daily in Victorian surroundings and is a local favourite.

Jamie's Italian ££ *1 George Square, tel: 0141-404 2690*, www. jamieoliver.com/italian. Open daily for lunch and dinner. Housed in a stylish conversion, Jamie Oliver's Italian-style restaurant offers honest Italian rustic seasonal fare.

Ox and Finch ££ *920 Sauchiehall Street, 0141-339 8627*, www.oxand finch.com. Open daily lunch and dinner. In a trendy part of town, this sharing-plate restaurant offers relaxed and rustic fine dining. The menu consists of a selection of tapas dishes and the dining area is bright and open.

La Parmigiana ££ *447 Great Western Road, tel: 0141-334 0686*, www.laparmigiana.co.uk. Open Monday–Saturday for lunch and dinner, also Sunday late lunch. This small, family-run establishment in Glasgow's west end serves Italian cuisine in elegant surroundings. The restaurant prides itself on the authenticity and excellence of its cuisine.

Red Onion ££ *257 West Campbell Street, tel: 0141-221 6000*, http:// red-onion.co.uk. Open daily lunch and dinner. Dishes are a modern twist on classic Scottish cooking, all delicately prepared. The spacious and relaxed space has mixed seating, including booths and a mezzanine.

Rogano £££ *11 Exchange Place, tel: 0141-248 4055*, www.rogano glasgow.com. Open daily for lunch and dinner. Open since 1935, this famous restaurant has an Art-Dec interior. It specialises in the freshest of seafood and has an excellent wine list. Downstairs, Café Rogano is a more informal, moderately priced restaurant. Reservations essential.

Willow Tea Rooms £ *217 Sauchiehall Street, tel: 0141-332 0521*, www.willowtearooms.co.uk. Open Monday–Saturday for breakfast, lunch and tea; Sunday for lunch and tea only. Charles Rennie Mackintosh's original tearooms (upstairs from the jewellery shop on the ground floor). Mackintosh designed the details of the building's interior. Recreated Willow Tea Rooms are at 97 Buchanan Street. Both serve the sandwiches, cakes and tea you would expect.

Windows £££ *In the Carlton George, 44 West George Street, 7th floor;* tel: 0141-354 5070, www.carlton.nl/george. Open daily for breakfast, lunch, pre-theatre meals and dinner. An excellent and attractive restaurant with interesting rooftop views. Only the freshest produce is used. It is advisable to book.

CENTRAL SCOTLAND

But 'n' Ben £ *Auchmithie,* tel: 01241-877223, www.butnbenauch mithie.co.uk. Open Wednesday–Monday for lunch, Monday and Wednesday–Saturday for dinner. This restaurant housed in a row of cottages is best-known for its high tea and inexpensive seafood dishes which are served in comfortable surroundings by friendly staff.

The Cellar £££ *24 East Green, Anstruther, Fife,* tel: 01333-310378, www.thecellaranstruther.co.uk. Open Thursday–Sunday for lunch, Wednesday–Sunday for dinner. This famed seafood restaurant located in the waterfront town of Anstruther has a menu that ranges from the renowned crayfish-and-mussel bisque to Scottish beef and lamb. Excellent wine list.

Clachan Inn £ *2 Main Street, Drymen,* tel: 01360-660824, www. clachaninndrymen.co.uk. Open daily for lunch and dinner. Very child-friendly, with special children's menu. Pub menu that includes fish and chips and hearty casseroles.

India on the Green ££ *9 Victoria Road, Ballater,* tel: 01339-755701, www.indiaonthegreen.co.uk. Open daily for lunch and dinner. For delicate cuisine from India and Bangladesh, with a Western twist, try this award-winning option.

The Kilberry Inn £££ *Kilberry Road, Kilberry,* tel: 01880-770223, www.kilberryinn.com. Open Thursday–Sunday for lunch, Tuesday–Sunday for dinner. It's worth seeking out this wonderful restaurant with rooms, reached by a single-track road between Tarbet and Lochgilphead. Scottish restaurant of the year in 2009, the local produce is used to wonderful effect.

Moon Fish Cafe £££ *9 Correction Wynd, Aberdeen, tel: 01224 644166*, www.moonfishcafe.co.uk. Open Tuesday–Saturday for lunch and dinner. Tucked away among Aberdeen's medieval streets, the changing menu brings up-and-coming food trends from around the world to the table. Friendly staff create an unpretentious atmosphere.

Old Boatyard ££ *Fishmarket Quay, Arbroath, tel: 01241-879995*, www.oldboatyard.co.uk. Open daily for lunch and tea. An attractive modern building, which retains a traditional feel, the restaurant is located in Arbroath's newly developed harbour. Seafood is a favourite, but there are plenty of other tasty choices.

Peat Inn £££ *By Cupar, Fife, tel: 01334-840206*, www.thepeatinn. co.uk. Open Tuesday–Saturday for lunch and dinner. A pioneer in the revival of Scottish cuisine, this restaurant is a dining experience. Reservations recommended. If you want to stay here as well, the inn has 8 rooms; book well in advance.

The Seafood Restaurant £££ *Bruce Embankment, St Andrews tel: 01334-479475*, www.theseafoodrestaurant.com. Open daily for lunch and dinner. Where better to eat seafood than in this classy restaurant with a beautiful view over the water. Serves up lobster, prawns, scallops and much more.

The Silver Darling £££ *Pocra Quay, Aberdeen, tel: 01224-576229*, www.thesilverdarling.co.uk. Open Monday–Friday for lunch, Monday–Saturday for dinner. Superb seafood that varies depending on the daily catch. 'Silver Darling' is the local nickname for herring.

HIGHLANDS AND ISLANDS

Badachro Inn ££ *By Gairloch, tel: 01445-741255*, www.badachroinn. com. Open daily for lunch and dinner. Delightful setting overlooking Loch Gairloch for this popular pub with a plesant garden. The daily changing menus highlight locally caught seafood and there is a wide choice of real ale, wine or malt whisky.

Bosville Restaurant ££ *In the Bosville Hotel, Portree, Skye, tel: 01478-612846*, www.bosvillehotel.co.uk. Open daily for lunch and dinner. Serving bistro-style food where fresh local seafood is a speciality, as are Aberdeen Angus beef and game. The dishes are seasoned with locally grown herbs and accompanied by local organic vegetables. Reservations are a must.

Café 1 ££ *75 Castle Street, Inverness, tel: 01463-226200*, www.cafe1. net. Open Monday–Saturday for lunch and dinner. Located in the town centre, this well-reputed restaurant offers new Scottish cuisine. Reservations recommended.

Creelers Arran ££ *Home Farm, Brodick, Arran, tel: 01770 302810*, www.creelers.co.uk. Open Tuesday–Saturday for lunch and dinner. Renowned fish restaurant featuring seafood that comes from Arran, which is smoked on site at the owners own smokehouse.

The Three Chimneys ££££ *Colbost (near Dunvegan), Skye, tel: 01470-511258*, www.threechimneys.co.uk. Open Monday–Saturday lunch, daily dinner. Check opening times in winter. This is an award-winning restaurant that offers fine food using local ingredients in charming surroundings. Five-star rooms are also available if you want to stay overnight.

A–Z TRAVEL TIPS

A Summary of Practical Information

A

ACCOMMODATION (see also Camping, Youth Hostels and Recommended Hotels)

There is a great variety of accommodation in Scotland: hotels, guest houses, manor houses, castles and bed-and-breakfasts. The Scottish Tourist Board inspects and grades many of these establishments. There are also hundreds of self-catering cottages, caravans, chalets and crofts (small farmhouses). Farmhouse holidays and accommodation in private homes are other possibilities. The tourist office can supply information about all these options.

Hotels vary greatly in standards. Many of the most pleasant are converted country mansions in isolated settings. Some hotels have swimming pools, and quite a few have their own golf courses.

Book ahead for Easter, and July–September. Most tourist offices offer 'local bed-booking' services that assure overnight accommodation on the same day. You pay a minimal deposit for the reservation, which is deducted from your bill. Some tourist boards also charge a small booking fee.

VisitScotland (www.visitscotland.com) lists hotels that have special facilities for disabled visitors and young children, and those that offer low-season prices for senior citizens.

Guest houses and bed-and-breakfast (B&B) premises can be great bargains, although you'll sometimes have to share a bathroom. Most establishments have a restaurant or can arrange for an evening meal.

AIRPORTS

Scotland has four major airports – Glasgow, Edinburgh, Prestwick and Aberdeen – and many regional airports scattered about on the mainland and the islands that are served by Loganair.

Glasgow Airport (www.glasgowairport.com) handles much of Scotland's air traffic. It is a 9-mile (15km), 20-minute taxi or bus ride from the city centre. Buses, including the Glasgow Airport Shuttle, travel every 10–30 minutes between the airport and Buchanan bus station in central Glasgow. Buses from the Buchanan station travel to Edinburgh (about 70 minutes) and other destinations in Scotland.

Edinburgh Airport (www.edinburghairport.com) handles UK, European and a couple of transatlantic services, but is beginning to rival Glasgow in receiving international flights. The airport is 7 miles (11km) from Edinburgh, and is linked with Waverley railway station at Waverley Bridge, in the city centre by a special Airlink bus service that leaves every 10 minutes and takes about 30 minutes. A tram also runs from the airport to the city (York Place). Taxis are available just outside the arrival hall.

Prestwick Airport (www.glasgowprestwick.com), about one hour from Glasgow (32 miles/51km), handles European and domestic flights. The modern terminal has its own train station, with services to Glasgow approximately every 20 minutes. Public buses run to Glasgow and destinations in Ayrshire.

Aberdeen Airport (www.aberdeenairport.com), a 7-mile (11km), 35-minute bus ride from Aberdeen station, serves mainly British and European destinations.

B

BICYCLE HIRE

Scotland offers many cycling opportunities. Local firms at tourist resorts will rent bicycles by the hour, day, or week. The Scottish Tourist Board list many rental firms on their website (www.visitscotland.com). Book ahead for July or August. See page 90 for information about biking trails.

BUDGETING FOR YOUR TRIP

Although good value for money is still the general rule in Scotland, bargains are rare and inflation relentlessly does its familiar work.
Accommodation: Double in moderately priced hotel with breakfast,

£60–70 per person. Double per person in guest house with breakfast £40–50. Bed-and-breakfast (without bath), £30–40 per person.

Airport transfer: Edinburgh: bus £4 (£7 return), taxi about £25. Glasgow: bus (Glasgow Shuttle) £6.50 (£9 return), taxi £22; Citylink bus between Edinburgh city centre and Glasgow Airport (standard ticket) £13.80 (£17.20 return).

Bicycle hire: £15–17 per day, £70–80 per week.

Buses: Edinburgh–Glasgow (standard tickets) £7.50 (£11.40 return). Explorer Pass: 3 days £41; 16 days (8 days of travel) £93; www.city link.co.uk. City and local buses: fares can depend on distance. Minimum bus fare in Edinburgh is £1.50 and £4 for 3 or more journeys in a day. Glasgow bus fares start at £1.20; exact fare is required.

Campsites: £15–20 per tent per night.

Meals: Lunch in pub or café £8–12; moderately priced restaurant meal with wine £24–30; afternoon tea £7; a pint of beer ranges from £2.70–3.50.

Shopping: Pure wool tartan, about £46 per metre; cashmere scarf, from around £35; kilt: man's from £250, woman's from £125; cashmere sweater from £100; lambswool sweater £25–40.

Sights: Most museums are free. Edinburgh Castle adult £16.50, child £9.90.

Taxis: Basic rate (Edinburgh) for two passengers begins at £2.10; increases by 25p every 210m/yds until 11.30pm, then for every 242m/yds; 20p extra for each additional passenger.

Tours: City on-and-off bus tours £14; sightseeing day tours from £14; cruises from one hour to full day £12–40.

Trains: Prices vary according to day or time of travel. Glasgow–Edinburgh £12.50 off-peak travel one way. Freedom of Scotland pass (accepted on trains, buses and most ferries): 8 days (4 days of travel) £134, 15 days (8 days of travel) £179.70. Saver one-way fares (on ScotRail services only and bought at least one day in advance): London–Edinburgh £66.50; Edinburgh–Inverness £21.30; Glasgow–Aberdeen £11.30; www.scotrail.co.uk.

C

CAMPING

There are more than 600 campsites in Scotland. The most elaborate have hot showers, flush toilets, laundry facilities and shops and can offer nature trails, forest walks and even access to golf courses. Many sites are more basic, with just a handful of pitches. To camp or caravan on private land you must have the owner's permission.

See VisitScotland's website (www.visitscotland.com) for more information. Some of the most attractive locations are operated by the Forestry Commission; for more information visit http://scotland.forestry.gov.uk or www.campingintheforest.co.uk for a comprehensive list of their camp sites.

CAR HIRE

As a rule, it is cheaper to book a hire car before you leave on your trip. Be sure to check whether your credit card covers insurance. A medium-sized compact family car £240 per week, £48 per day, including vat, unlimited mileage, but not insurance. Prices vary widely according to season. Beware hidden extras.

To hire a car you must be 21 or more years of age and have held a driver's licence for at least 12 months. Valid drivers' licences from almost all countries are recognised by the British authorities.

Major car rental companies are: Avis, tel: 0844-581 0147, www.avis.co.uk; Budget, tel: 0844-544 3407, www.budget.co.uk; Europcar, tel: 0871 384 9900, www.europcar.co.uk; Hertz, tel: 0870-844 8844, www.hertz.co.uk. For competitive rates, try Arnold Clark, tel: 0141-237 4374, www.arnoldclarkrental.com.

CLIMATE

The best months to visit Scotland are May and June, which have the most hours of sunshine and comparatively little rain. There aren't many of the midges and other stinging insects that become a problem, especially on the west coast, in full summer.

Average monthly temperatures are as follows:

	J	F	M	A	M	J	J	A	S	O	N	D
°C	4	5	7	10	14	17	19	18	15	11	7	6
°F	39	41	44	50	58	62	66	64	59	52	44	43

CLOTHING

Even if you're holidaying in Scotland in midsummer, take warm clothing and rainwear. Anoraks are very useful: buy a bright colour to make yourself conspicuous to hunters if you're going to be hiking or climbing. Sturdy shoes are a must both for outdoor walking and traversing cobblestone streets.

Scotland makes some of the world's best clothing, and you'll find a fine selection of knits, woollens and tweeds, although not at significantly lower prices than elsewhere in the UK.

CRIME AND SAFETY

As everywhere, crime in Scotland can be a problem, but even Glasgow, with Scotland's highest crime rate, is not dangerous by world standards. Take all the usual precautions. Honesty, however, is still quite prevalent in Scotland, even in the cities.

D

DRIVING

Road Conditions. A limited number of motorways connect Glasgow and Edinburgh with other major cities and areas. Be aware that most A roads are winding, two-lane roads, often skirting Scotland's many lochs and they can be slow-going. A surprise to most visitors are the single-lane roads found in the hinterland and on the islands. Most of these are paved, with passing places for giving way to oncoming traffic or allowing cars behind you to overtake (thank the driver who pulls over for you). Obviously, you should never park in these essential passing places. The twisting roads, along with the need for pulling in and out of the side slips, will more than double your normal driving time even over short distances. Other obstacles include sheep and cattle that often wander onto minor roads. Signposting is adequate, but a good map is essential.

Rules and regulations. The same basic rules apply in all of Britain. Drive on the left, overtake on the right. Turn left on a roundabout (traffic circle); at a junction where no road has priority, yield to traffic coming from the right. Seat belts must be worn. Drinking and driving is regarded as a serious offence and penalties are severe, involving loss of licence, heavy fines, and even prison sentences, and the law is strictly enforced.

To bring a car into Scotland you'll need registration and insurance papers and a driver's licence. Overseas visitors driving their own cars will need Green Card insurance as well.

Speed limits. In built-up areas, 30 or 40mph (48 or 65kmh); on major roads, 60mph (96kmh); on dual carriageways and motorways, 70mph (112kmh).

Fuel. Petrol is sold by the Imperial gallon (about 20 percent more voluminous than the US gallon) and by the litre; pumps show both measures. Four-star grade is 97 octane and three-star is 94 octane. Unleaded petrol and diesel is widely available. Most petrol stations are self-service. In the more remote areas stations are rather scarce, so take advantage when you see one.

If you need help. Members of automobile clubs that are affiliated with the British Automobile Association (AA) or the Royal Automobile Club (RAC) can benefit from speedy, efficient assistance in the event of a breakdown. If this should happen to you, AA members should tel: 0800-887 766, RAC members tel: 0800-828 282. Green Flag Motoring Assistance, tel: 0800-051 0636, (free to members or you may join on the spot).

Parking. There are meters in major centres and vigilant corps of traffic police and wardens to ticket violators, even in small towns. Ticket machines take most coins and some now take credit cards. Do not park on double yellow lines.

In Edinburgh and Glasgow, your car is best left in a car park. Concert Square, next to Buchanan bus station in Glasgow, has a large multistorey car park. In Edinburgh, Castle Terrace is a large multistorey car park near Edinburgh Castle; St James' Centre (enter on York Place) is at the east end of Princes Street.

Road signs. Many standard international picture signs are displayed in Scotland. Distances are shown in miles. In the Highlands and islands only, road signs may appear first in Gaelic, then English.

E

ELECTRICITY

Throughout Scotland it's 230 volts AC, 50 Hz. Certain appliances may need a converter. Americans will need an adapter.

EMBASSIES AND CONSULATES

Many countries have consuls or other representatives in Edinburgh, but others only have representation in London.

Australia: Australian High Commission, Australia House, Strand, London WC2B 4LA, tel: 020 7420 3690.

Canada: Canadian Consulate, tel: 07702 359916, email: canada. consul.edi@gmail.com.

US: American Consulate General, 3 Regent Terrace, Edinburgh EH7 5BN; tel: 0131-556 8315.

EMERGENCIES

To call the fire brigade, police, ambulance, coast guard, lifeboat, or mountain rescue service, dial 999 from any telephone. You need no coin. Tell the emergency operator which service you need.

G

GAY AND LESBIAN TRAVELLERS

Scotland is a conservative country and the gay scene is found primarily in Edinburgh and Glasgow; both have lively gay pubs and nightclubs. The centre of Edinburgh's gay community is Broughton Street at the east end of town. Support is offered by the LGBT Helpline Scotland (tel: 0131-556 4049; www.lgbt-helpline-scotland.org.uk). The monthly magazine *Scotsgay* has a useful website (www.scotsgay.co.uk).

GETTING THERE

By air.

From North America. Direct transatlantic flights to Glasgow from Toronto are offered by Canadian Affair and Air Transat (Toronto, Calgary, Vancouver; US Airways (Philadelphia and Orlando), United (Newark, NJ). Flights from a variety of US hubs route flights via London or Amsterdam.

From Australia and New Zealand. Qantas offer non-direct flights from Sydney and Melbourne to London. Air New Zealand has daily flights to London from Auckland.

From England and Republic of Ireland. There are direct services from all parts of the UK on British Airways, flybe, EasyJet and Ryanair, including frequent departures from Birmingham, Heathrow, Gatwick, Stansted, Southampton, Bristol and Manchester. Aer Lingus and Ryanair have regular flights from Dublin.

From Europe. Air France, KLM, Lufthansa, Ryanair and EasyJet have direct flights from continental Europe to either Glasgow, Edinburgh or Aberdeen.

Air fares. The highest air fares are from June to September; fares in other months of the year may be considerably lower. All airlines offer economy fares: PEX, APEX, etc. These are subject to restrictions – for example, APEX flights have to be booked at least 14 days in advance and tickets are not refundable.

From the US, a direct flight to London with a domestic flight to Glasgow may be the cheapest option. Many American airlines offer a variety of package deals, both for group travel and for those who wish to travel independently. Packages include airfare, accommodation and travel between holiday destinations and may include some meals.

By rail. The train journey from London King's Cross to Edinburgh takes 4.5 hours, and from London Euston to Glasgow takes 5.5 hours. A sleeper service is available from London (Euston) to Glasgow, Edinburgh, Aberdeen, Inverness and Fort William.

Visitors can take advantage of a variety of special fare plans that operate in Scotland. The **Freedom of Scotland Travelpass** is available for either 4 days of travel over 8 consecutive days, or 8 days of travel over 15 consecutive days. The pass gives unlimited travel on many bus routes and Caledonian MacBrayne (www.calmac.co.uk) ferries as well as on Scotland's rail network. It can be purchased at ScotRail stations or online (www.scotrail.co.uk), and at selected English travel centres. Travelpass holders can obtain a 20 percent reduction on NorthLink sailings from Aberdeen or Stromness to Orkney and Shetland. You can also choose from a selection of Rail Rover tickets; enquire at railway stations.

Visitors from abroad who wish to tour by rail can buy a **BritRail Pass** www.britrail.net before leaving their home countries. These offer unlimited travel on the railway network throughout Scotland, England and Wales during a consecutive period of 2, 4, 8, 15 or 22 days, or a month. The **Flexipass** allows journeys to be made on non-consecutive days; for example, 4 days unlimited travel over an 8-day period. Children aged 5 to 15 pay half price. The **BritRail Youth Pass** is for youngsters aged 16–25. None of these can be purchased in Britain.

By road. From London the quickest route is to take the M1 north to connect with the A1. If you are in the west, the M5 merges with the M6 and connects with the M74 to Glasgow.

To take your own car to Scotland, you will need proof of ownership and insurance documents, including Green Card insurance.

There are frequent coach services from all over Britain to various Scottish destinations by **National Express** (www.nationalexpress.com) and **Scottish Citylink** (www.citylink.co.uk).

By sea. Ferry services from Northern Ireland operate from Larne to Troon and Belfast to Stranraer.

GUIDES AND TOURS

Dozens of bus tours are available in Scotland. Scotline Tours (www.scotlinetours.co.uk) and Timberbush Tours (www.timberbush-tours.co.uk), based in Edinburgh, offer three-, two- and one-tours to St Andrews, Loch Lomond, Loch Ness, the Borders and other destinations; Gray Line (www.graylinetours.com) and Glasgow-based Scottish Tours (www.scottishtours.co.uk) offer similar options. All tours can be booked through the tourist information offices, at Princes Mall in Edinburgh and George Square in Glasgow. Tour operators, centres, and hotels provide package holidays for sports such as golf and other outdoor sports.

Both Glasgow and Edinburgh have a number of city hop-on-hop-off bus tours. Tours originate at George Square in Glasgow (www.cityxplora.com /locations/glasgow) and at St Andrew Square in Edinburgh (www.hop-on-hop-off-bus.com/edinburgh-bus-tours).

Details of guides and tours can also be had from The Secretary, Scottish Tour Guides Association, Norrie's House, 18b Broad Street, Stirling, FK8 1EF, tel: 01786-447784; www.stga.co.uk. Members of this association wear official badges engraved with their names. Most are based in Edinburgh, Glasgow, Aberdeen and Dundee. Some will accompany tours.

H

HEALTH AND MEDICAL CARE

Scotland, home of much pioneering work in medicine, is proud of the high standard of its health care. Medical care is free for EU (on production of the EHIC card) and Commonwealth residents under the National Health Service (NHS). Other nationals should check to be sure they have adequate health insurance coverage. US residents should be aware that Medicare does not apply outside the United States.

Emergency care. Major hospitals with 24-hour emergency service are: Edinburgh Royal Infirmary, tel: 0131-536 1000; Glasgow Royal Infirmary, tel: 0141-211 4000; Aberdeen Royal Infirmary, tel: 0845-456 6000; and Inverness Raigmore, tel: 01463-704000.

Pharmacies. In Edinburgh, Glasgow and a few other major centres you should find a duty chemist (drugstore) open until 9pm; otherwise, contact a police station for help in filling in an emergency prescription, or dial 999.

Insects. In the summer midges are a nuisance or worse, especially on Scotland's west coast. Clegs (horse flies) and tiny but devilish berry bugs also attack in warmer weather. Insect repellents aren't always effective; ask the advice of a chemist.

L

LANGUAGE

Gaelic and old Scottish words and phrases in everyday use will baffle the most fluent English speaker. Today just over 60,000 Scots speak Gaelic, most of them residents of the Western Isles. English spoken with a strong Scots accent can take a while to get used to and place names are often not pronounced the way you'd expect: Kirkcudbright is *Kircoobree*, Culzean is *Cullane*, Colquhoun is *Cohoon*, Culross is *Coorus*, Menzies is *Mingies*, Dalziell is *Dee-ell*.

Scottish/Gaelic **English**
aber **river mouth**
Auld Reekie **Edinburgh (Old Smoky)**
ben **mountain**

bide a wee **wait a bit**
biggin **building**
brae **hillside**
bramble **blackberry**
brig **bridge**
burn **stream**
ceilidh **song/story gathering**
clachan **hamlet**
croft **small land-holding**
dinna fash yersel' **don't get upset**
eilean **island**
firth **estuary**
gait **street**
ghillie **attendant to hunting or fishing**
haud yer wheesht **shut up**
inver **mouth of river**
ken **know**
kirk **church**
kyle **strait, narrows**
lang may yer lum reek **long may your chimney smoke (i.e. may you have a long life)**
link **dune**
linn **waterfall**
mickle **small amount**
mull **promontory**
ness **headland**
provost **mayor**
sett **tartan pattern**
skirl **shriek of bagpipes**
strath **river valley**
thunderplump **thunderstorm**
wynd **lane, alley**

M

MAPS

Free maps and helpful directions are available at any tourism office. For driving, a good map is essential. The Collins *Touring Map of Scotland* is published in association with VisitScotland. Collins also publishes street atlases of Edinburgh and Glasgow and the *A–Z Street Atlas* is available for both cities. Route maps for hiking and biking are available from the tourist office; you may also want to buy one of the series of ordinance maps that are available.

MEDIA

Television: Viewers in Scotland have plenty of choice with two main BBC channels and several commercial channels. Digital television services provide a wide range of extra channels. Many larger hotels offer a variety of cable and satellite TV channels and pay-per-view films.

Radio: Radio Scotland is the main BBC radio service and national BBC radio stations also operate in Scotland. A range of commercial radio stations cater for different areas of Scotland. Various international stations can also be received.

Newspapers and magazines: In addition to British national newspapers, Scottish daily papers are: the *Herald* (published in Glasgow), the *Scotsman* (published in Edinburgh), the *Daily Record*, and the *Aberdeen Press and Journal*. Details of events and entertainment in and around Glasgow and Edinburgh are given in the magazine *The List* (www.list.co.uk), published every two months. *The International Herald Tribune*, edited in Paris, and US weekly news magazines are sold in the major centres and at airports.

MONEY

Currency. The pound sterling (£) is a decimal monetary unit and is divided into 100 pence (p). Coins consist of 1p, 2p, 5p, 10p, 20p, 50p, £1 and £2; and banknotes consist of £1 (a few Scottish notes are still in circulation), £5, £10, £20, £50, and £100.

Scottish banks issue their own notes, which are not, technically, legal tender in England and Wales, although many shops will accept them and English banks will readily change them for you.

Currency exchange. You will get the best exchange rate for your foreign currency at banks (see Opening Hours); currency exchange bureaux rarely offer as good a rate, and you'll get the worst rate at your hotel. Many Tourist Information Offices have currency exchange facilities.

Credit cards. Major credit cards are widely accepted in hotels, restaurants, petrol stations and shops, although not always in small guesthouses and B&Bs – signs are usually displayed indicating which are accepted.

Travellers' cheques. Travellers' cheques are accepted throughout Scotland. You'll need your passport when cashing them, and banks will charge a fee. The American Express office will cash its own travellers' cheques without a fee.

O

OPENING HOURS

Opening hours may vary from place to place. However, **banks** are usually open Monday–Friday 9am–5pm, with branches in city centres open on Saturday mornings. Banks in small towns may close for lunch. Some rural areas are served only by mobile banks that arrive at regular intervals and stay for a few hours.

Offices and businesses are usually open Monday–Friday 9am–5pm; some have Saturday hours.

Post offices are open Monday–Friday 9am–5.30pm and Saturday 9am–12.30pm. Sub-stations have a half-day closing on Wednesday or Thursday.

Shop hours are normally Monday–Saturday 9am–5.30pm, some until 7pm or 8pm on Thursday. Some shops in villages and smaller towns close on Sunday and may close for lunch. In the larger cities in major shopping areas, shops open at either 11am or noon on Sunday and close at 5pm or 5.30pm.

Museums and sightseeing attractions have greatly varying opening hours. As a rule, attractions are open from about 9.30am until late afternoon, or early evening in summer. In winter many castles and other places of interest are closed to the public or open for limited periods. It's best to call for information. Museums in the cities are generally open Monday–Saturday 10am–5pm and noon–5pm on Sunday.

Major **tourist information offices** are open all year round, usually Monday–Saturday 9am–8pm and Sunday 10am–8pm in July and August. At other times of the year, they close earlier.

P

POLICE

Scottish police do not carry guns. Police patrol cars usually have yellow stripes and a blue light.

The emergency telephone number for police aid is **999** all over the country. You can also dial 0 and ask for the police.

POST OFFICES

Letters and packages sent within the UK can use the first- or second-class postal service. Because second-class mail may be slow, it's advisable to pay the modest extra postage for first class. Postcards and letters to Europe and elsewhere overseas automatically go by airmail. The post office offers an express mail service, Parcelforce International.

Stamps are sold at post offices (found in almost every Scottish village even if they share space with grocery shops) and newsagents, as well as from vending machines. Postboxes are red and come in many shapes and sizes.

Edinburgh's main post office is in Princes Mall Shopping Centre, Waverley Bridge (tel: 0131-524 6901). Glasgow's main post office is 47 St Vincent Street, tel: 0141-531 7511.

Postage: within the UK 62p; to Europe and the rest of world, airmail 97p.

PUBLIC HOLIDAYS

Bank holidays in Scotland are not always closing days for offices and shops. Many towns have their individual holidays, generally on a Monday. VisitScotland publishes an annual list of local and national holidays and the chart below is a guide to fixed holidays. If one falls on a Saturday or Sunday, it is usual to take off the following Monday.

1 January **New Year's Day**
2 January **Bank Holiday**
25 December **Christmas Day**
26 December **Boxing Day**
Moveable dates:
March or April **Good Friday/Easter Monday**
May **Spring Bank Holiday**
August **Summer Bank Holiday**

T

TELEPHONES

Public phones are located in pubs, restaurants, post offices, shops and in the street. BT booths can usually accept coins, phonecards or credit/debit cards. Internet kiosks are also available. Phonecards of various denominations can be purchased from newsagents, post offices and tourist information offices. Some phones in small towns and public buildings are still coin-operated.

Public phone booths display information on overseas dialling codes and the international exchange. Dial 118 505 for international directory inquiries, 155 for an international operator. Local directory enquiries are provided by several companies - numbers include 118 500, 118 365, 118 212 and 118 118, and for operator assistance, dial 100. To make a local reverse-charge call, dial 100 and ask the operator to reverse the charges.

Mobile (cell) phone coverage is not as good in Scotland as the rest of the UK, with rural areas particularly neglected by service providers. Edinburgh, however, has good coverage, including 4G. Coverage varies extensively between different mobile phone companies. You will need a GSM cellular phone for use in Scotland. It is possible to rent these but this is an expensive option, especially for a short stay. If you have a GSM phone the roaming charges may well be high. The cheapest option is to buy a local UK SIM card to use in the GSM phone; incoming calls will be free and local calls inexpensive. Check out all the options before travelling.

TIME ZONES

Scotland, like the rest of the United Kingdom, is on Greenwich Mean Time. Between April and October clocks are put forward one hour.

New York	**Edinburgh**	Jo'burg	Sydney	Auckland
7am	**noon**	1pm	9pm	11pm

TIPPING

While tipping is customary in Scotland, there's no pressure. Hotels and restaurants may add a service charge to your bill, in which case tipping is not really necessary. If service is not included, add about 10 percent to your bill. Many cafés and informal restaurants have a box for tips beside the cash register.

Tip hotel porters about £1 per bag, and tip your hotel maid about £5 per week. Lavatory attendants should get 20–50p. Your taxi driver will be pleased with 10 percent, and so will your tour guide. Hairdressers should get 10–20 percent.

TOURIST INFORMATION

There is probably no tourist destination in the world that produces more information for visitors than Scotland. Strategically placed throughout the Lowlands, Highlands and Islands are some 150 tourist information centres, offering a wide range of publications, free or for sale, as well as expert advice. For a complete list of their addresses, write to the headquarters of VisitScotland at the address below. They're identified by blue-and-white signs with an italicised i (for 'information').

In Edinburgh the **Tourist Information Centre** is in Princes Street Mall, 3 Princes Street, tel: 0845-225 5121, or there's an Information and Accommodation Service at Edinburgh Airport. In Glasgow, the information centre is at 170 Buchanan Street; tel: 0845 859 1006.

The national headquarters of **VisitScotland** (www.visitscotland. com) is at Ocean Point One, 94 Ocean Drive, Edinburgh; tel: 0131-524 2121. Don't turn up here for help; only written and telephone inquiries are accepted. National tourist information can be supplied by any major tourist information centre in Scotland. For further information on Scotland and the rest of Britain check www.visit britain.com. In London you can drop into the City of London Visitor Centre, St Paul's Churchyard, London EC4M 8BY; tel: 020-7332 1456.

TRANSPORT

Scotland's extensive public transport network can be of considerable use to tourists. If you're touring the north without a car, a Travelpass (see page 122) enables you to travel on most coaches, trains and ferries operating in the Highlands and Islands at a significant saving. Maps, timetables and brochures are available free from tourist offices and transport terminals (see page 131). There are also money-saving excursions, weekend and island-to-island ferry schemes. On the Western Isles post buses are scheduled to link up with ferry services.

City transport. Most Scottish towns and cities have good bus services, particularly Edinburgh and Glasgow. Night bus services in cities are less frequent. Family and other discount tickets are available in Edinburgh at the Lothian Buses Travelshop at Waverley Bridge (tel: 0131-333 3708; www.lothianbuses.com). The First Bus (www.firstgroup.com/ukbus/scotland_east) company serves urban and rural areas around Edinburgh. In Glasgow, the main bus company is First Bus; contact the Travel Centre at Buchanan bus station, Killermont Street.

Edinburgh Trams (tel: 0131-555 6363; www.edinburghtrams.com) work in partnership with Lothian Buses. Trams run for 15 stops between York Place in New Town and Edinburgh Airport.

Glasgow also has a simple but efficient subway system, nicknamed 'the Clockwork Orange', which operates in the city centre. The Park and Ride scheme involves parking your car at certain underground stations on the outskirts of the city and then taking the subway into the centre.

Coaches. Comfortable and rapid long-distance coaches with toilets link the major towns. For details, call **National Express** (tel: 0871-781 8181; www.nationalexpress.com); **Scottish Citylink** (tel: 0871-266 3333; www.citylink.co.uk) or **Buchanan Street Bus Station** (tel: 0141-333 3708). Citylink offers the Explorer Pass for three days' travel out of five, five days' travel out of ten or eight days out of 16, good on both major and local routes.

Trains. Train services include the InterCity trains, with principal routes from London to Glasgow's Central Station (5.5 hours) and to Edinburgh's Waverley Station (4.5 hours); there are day and night trains. From Glasgow's Queen Street Station, routes continue on to Perth, Dundee, Aberdeen and Inverness and there are smaller, secondary lines. For **National Rail Enquiries**, call 0845-748 4950 or visit www.nationalrail.co.uk.

Ferries. Ferries to the Western Isles are generally run by **Caledonian MacBrayne** (tel: 0800-066 3000; www.calmac.co.uk), North-Link Ferries, (tel: 0845-600 0449; www.northlinkferries.co.uk), connect with Orkney and Shetland; there are ferry services from

Aberdeen to Lerwick and from Scrabster to Stromness. There are also many ferries between the islands. Reservations are essential in peak season for the more popular car ferries.

Taxis. In Scotland's major centres you'll find most taxis are black, London-style cabs. A taxi's yellow 'For Hire' sign is lit when it's available for hire. There are taxi ranks at airports and stations, and you can hail them on the street. Major centres have 24-hour radio taxi services. There's an extra charge for luggage. If you hire a taxi for a long-distance trip, negotiate the price with the driver before setting off.

TRAVELLERS WITH DISABILITIES

Capability Scotland is Scotland's leading disability organisation, providing a range of flexible services which support disabled people of all ages in their everyday lives. Contact: Capability Scotland, 11 Ellersly Road, Edinburgh EH12 6HY (tel: 0131-337 9876; www.capability-scotland.org.uk).

V

VISAS AND ENTRY REQUIREMENTS

For non-British citizens the same formalities apply at Scottish ports of entry as elsewhere in the UK. Citizens of EU countries need only an identity card. Visitors from the US and most Commonwealth countries need only a valid passport for stays of up to 6 months.

On arrival at a British port or airport, if you have goods to declare you follow the red channel; with nothing to declare you take the green route, bypassing inspection, although customs officers may make random spot checks. Free exchange of non-duty-free goods for personal use is permitted between EU countries and the UK. Duty-free items are still subject to restrictions: check before you go. There's no limit on the amount of currency you can bring into or take out of Britain.

WEBSITES AND INTERNET ACCESS

The following are some useful websites for planning your visit.

Tourism

www.visitbritain.com British Tourist Authority

https://peoplemakeglasgow.com Greater Glasgow and Clyde Valley

www.thisisedinburgh.com Local guide to Edinburgh

www.undiscoveredscotland.co.uk Undiscovered Scotland

www.scotland.org.uk Travel Scotland

www.visitscotland.com Visit Scotland

General

www.historic-scotland.gov.uk Historic Scotland

www.nts.org.uk National Trust for Scotland

www.eventscotland.org Forthcoming festivals and sports events

www.scotsman.com *The Scotsman*

Scotland is well serviced when it comes to internet access, with even some of the remotest locations supported by dial-up, broadband or even Wi-fi. Larger towns and cities in Scotland have internet cafés and you will increasingly find hotels and guest houses offer internet and wireless access; many B&Bs are slowly following suit. Public libraries across Scotland offer free internet access and airports have computers available to access the internet, as well as Wi-fi hotspots.

YOUTH HOSTELS

The **Scottish Youth Hostels Association** runs around 70 hostels. Visitors can stay without being members of the association but membership brings many benefits, including reduced prices for rooms. Their address is 7 Glebe Crescent, Stirling FK8 2J (tel: 01786-891 400 or 0845-293 77373 for reservations; www.syha.org.uk). Hostels are graded by the VisitScotland quality assurance scheme.

RECOMMENDED HOTELS

Accommodation around Scotland covers a wide spectrum, from the basic B&B (bed-and-breakfast) to modern luxury hotels and ancient refurbished castles. VisitScotland (www.visitscotland.com) publishes many brochures and booklets detailing available accommodation, prices, facilities, etc.

Below you will find a selection of accommodation chosen for its quality and value for money. Prices are based on two people sharing a double room with breakfast in high season. Keep in mind that prices vary according to time of year and availability. All rooms have bath or shower and all establishments take major credit cards unless otherwise indicated. Edinburgh is extremely busy during the Edinburgh Festival (August), so book well in advance if you plan to visit the capital during that period.

££££	over £250
£££	£175–£250
££	£100–£175
£	below £100

EDINBURGH

The Balmoral ££££ *1 Princes St, EH2 2EQ, tel: 0131-556 2414,* www.roccofortehotels.com. This grand hotel has long been a legend. In a commanding position at the east end of Princes Street, it has a distinguished

Channings Hotel ££ *12–16 South Learmouth Gardens, EH4 1EZ, tel: 0131-315 2226,* www.channings.co.uk. This hotel, in a tranquil residential setting, suggests a Scottish country house. It has a notable restaurant, and is about five minutes by bus or car from the city centre. Also bar serving meals, and a sun-deck garden. 42 rooms.

The Glasshouse Hotel £££ *2 Greenside Place, EH1 3AA, tel: 0131-525 8200,* www.theglasshousehotel.co.uk. Situated near the east end of Princes Street, this is a state-of-the-art building where the rooms surround a 2-acre (0.8-hectare) roof garden. The exterior rooms have splendid views to the New Town or across the Firth of Forth. The Observatory restaurant offers great views over Carlton Hill. 77 rooms.

G&V Royal Mile Hotel ££££ *1 George Bridge, EH1 1AD, tel: 0131-220 6666, www.quorvuscollection.com.* Perfectly placed on Edinburgh's Royal Mile, this splendid luxurious boutique hotel certainly has the wow factor. Fabulous design and stunning use of bold textiles. 136 rooms.

Ibis Edinburgh Centre South Bridge ££ *77 South Bridge EH1 1HN, tel: 0131-292 0000, www.ibis.com.* Rising from the ashes of the Cowgate fire, this is not just another chain hotel. The decor is impeccable and the rooms have extremely comfortable beds Well located close to the Royal Mile. 259 rooms.

The Inn on the Mile ££ *82 High Street EH1 1LL,* tel: 0131-556 9940, www.theinnonthemile.co.uk. You'll find boutique-style bedrooms with attention to detail and comfort in this lovely old pub that's just a short walk from the castle. You can even join the weekly quiz on a Monday evening. 9 rooms.

Waldorf Astoria – The Caledonian ££££ *Princes Street, EH1 2AB, tel: 0131-222 8888, www.waldorfastoriaedinburgh.com.* One of the city's landmarks, this traditional luxury hotel is at the western end of bustling Princes Street, with views of Edinburgh Castle. Modern Scottish cuisine. Some rooms are adapted for disabled visitors. 241 rooms.

SOUTHEAST AND THE BORDERS

Burts Hotel ££ *Market Square, Melrose, TD6 9PN, tel: 01896-822 285, www.burtshotel.co.uk.* This family-run hotel is housed in a restored 1722 town house near the abbey. Rooms are airy and restful and the dining room serves good traditional Scottish food. Golf and fishing. 20 rooms.

Ednam House Hotel ££ *Bridge Street, Kelso, TD5 7HT, tel: 01573-224168, www.ednamhouse.com.* This large hotel on the River Tweed is housed in a mid-8th-century Georgian house; rooms have antiques and period furnishings. You can feast on good Scottish food while admiring the view of the river from the dining room. Golf and fishing, cycling paths and walks. 32 rooms.

Greywalls ££££ *Duncur Road, Muirfield, Gullane, East Lothian, EH31 2EG, tel: 01620-842144*, www.greywalls.co.uk. This attractive Edwardian house was designed by noted architect Sir Edwin Lutyens, with gardens laid out by Gertrude Jekyll. With fine views and an award-winning restaurant, it is a 40-minute drive from the centre of Edinburgh. On the edge of Muirfield championship golf course nearby. 23 rooms.

Hundalee House £ *Jedburgh, TD8 6PA, tel: 01835-063011*, email: sheila. whittaker@btinternet.com. This charming house is set in 15 acres (6 hectares) and perfect for touring the Borders region and just a mile from Jedburgh. You are guaranteed a warm welcome from the owners who have run this B&B for some 30 years. 4 rooms.

Knockinaam Lodge ££££ *Portpatrick, Dumfries and Galloway, DG9 9AD, tel: 01776-810471*, www.knockinaamlodge.com. Chic hunting-lodge-style Victorian hotel set in beautiful parkland. Fine sea views, excellent cuisine, fishing, superb walking. 10 luxury rooms.

GLASGOW

Angus Guest House £ *970 Sauchiehall Street, G3 7TH, tel: 0141-357 5155*, www.angushotelglasgow.co.uk. Near Kelvingrove Park and the art galleries, this small, friendly hotel is a good budget option where the staff are very helpful. 18 rooms.

Carlton George £££ *44 West George Street, G2 1DH, tel: 0141-353 6373*, www.carlton.nl/george. A modern, luxurious, state-of-the-art hotel in the heart of Glasgow. The Windows rooftop restaurant offers excellent Scottish cooking and great views. 64 rooms.

Grasshoppers Hotel ££ *87 Union Street, G1 3TA, tel: 0141-222 2666*, www.grasshoppersglasgow.com. Penthouse rooms above an office building close to the historic Glasgow Central station give great city views. It's surprisingly quiet here for its central location, and friendly staff and a wholesome breakfast make this a unique city experience. 30 rooms.

Malmaison ££ *278 West George Street, G2 4LL, tel: 0141-572 1000*, www.malmaison.com. Modern and trendy with beautifully decorated rooms, this former Greek Orthodox church still manages to preserve its important historical character. Restaurant serving British and French influenced cuisine. 72 rooms.

Hotel du Vin & Bistro £££ *1 Devonshire Gardens, G12 0UX, tel: 0141-339 2001*, www.hotelduvin.com. In a leafy district west of the centre, this luxury boutique hotel occupies a stunning Victorian terrace and offers beautifully decorated rooms and impeccable service. 49 rooms.

CENTRAL SCOTLAND

Apex City Quay Hotel and Spa £ *1 West Victoria Dock Road, Dundee, DD1 3JP, tel: 01382-202404*, www.apexhotels.co.uk. Located in the heart of the new City Quay development and overlooking the River Tay, this striking hotel is stylish and contemporary. Good food, plus spa, sauna and treament rooms. 151 rooms.

The Caledonian ££ *10–14 Union Terrace, Aberdeen, AB10 1WE, tel: 0871-376 9003*, www.thistle.com. Centrally located Victorian building with modern facilities and elegant public rooms; restaurant and café/wine bar. 83 rooms.

Dalmunzie Castle Hotel £££ *Spittal o' Glenshee, Blairgowrie, PH10 7QG, tel: 01250-885224*, www.dalmunzie.com. A mountain laird's mansion with splendid views, situated 18 miles (29km) north of Blairgowrie on the A93. Good home-cooking as well as fishing, golf and tennis. Conveniently located for the ski slopes. 17 rooms.

Easter Dunfallandy Country House ££ *Pitlochry, PH16 5NA, tel: 01796-474031*, www.dunfallandy.co.uk. Just 2 miles (3km) south of Pitlochry, this Georgian house overlooks the town and has stunning views of the Tummel Valley. Self-catering accommodation with use of kitchen, utility room, dining room and extensive gardens. 4 rooms.

The George Hotel £ *Main Street East, Inveraray PA32 8TT, tel: 01499-302111*, www.thegeorgehotel.co.uk. The George has been sensitively restored, with fine antiques and paintings a star feature. The pub part, with cocktail bar and conservatory restaurant, has stone floors and beamed ceilings. 17 rooms.

Kildrummy Castle Hotel ££ *Kildrummy by Alford, Aberdeenshire, AB33 8RA, tel: 01975-571288*, www.kildrummycastlehotel.com. Victorian country house in baronial-castle style near the old castle ruins and Kildrummy Gardens. Fine dining. 16 rooms.

Killiecrankie House Hotel £££ *Killiecrankie, Pitlochry, Perthshire, tel: 01796-473220*, www.killiecrankiehotel.co.uk. This country-house hotel, in a scenic setting, is a good base for touring the area. Excellent meals cooked by an award-winning chef. 10 rooms.

The Old Course Hotel ££££ *St Andrews, Fife KY16 9SP, tel: 01334-474371*, www.oldcoursehotel.co.uk. Modern luxury hotel bordering the historic golf course with good restaurants, indoor swimming pool, health spa and beauty salon. 102 rooms and 32 suites.

The Park Lodge Hotel £ *32 Park Terrace, Stirling, FK8 2JS, tel: 01786-474862*, www.parklodge.net. An elegant hotel in a part-Victorian, part-Georgian mansion overlooking the castle and park. Rooms are furnished with antiques, some four-poster beds. 9 rooms.

The Royal George Hotel ££ *Tay Street, Perth, RH1 5LD, tel: 01738-624455*, www.theroyalgeorgehotel.com. Beautifully located on the banks of the River Tay, The Royal George has been receiving visitors for over 230 years. Enjoy a traditional breakfast in the conservatory with fine views of the river. 45 rooms.

HIGHLANDS AND ISLANDS

The Arisaig Hotel ££ Main Road, *Arisaig, Inverness-shire, PH39 4NH, tel: 01687-450210*, www.arisaighotel.co.uk. Arisaig Hotel dates back to the Jacobite era, and was originally built as a coaching inn around 1720. The hotel looks across Arisaig Bay towards the Isles of Eigg and Muck. Varied menu. 13 rooms.

Bosville Hotel ££ *Bosville Terrace, Portree, Skye, IV51 9DG, tel: 01478-612846*, www.bosvillehotel.co.uk. Stylish accommodation with views of Portree Harbour and Cuillin Hills; outstanding bistro (see page 112). 15 rooms.

Craigmonie Hotel ££ *9 Annfield Road, Inverness, IV2 3HX, tel: 01463-231649*, www.craigmoniehotelinverness.co.uk. Situated in the heart of Inverness with the feel of a country dwelling, Craigmonie offers luxurious leisure activities and a delicious à la carte menu. 40 rooms.

Culloden House Hotel ££££ *Culloden, Inverness, IV1 7BZ, tel: 01463-790461*, www.cullodenhouse.co.uk. Georgian house close to the site of the 1746 battle, and 3 miles (5km) east of Inverness on the A96. Bonnie Prince Charlie slept here before the battle. Extensive gardens and parkland; facilities include tennis, sauna and solarium. Restaurant. 28 rooms.

Inverlochy Castle ££££ *Torlundy, Fort William, PH33 6SN, tel: 01397-702177*, www.inverlochycastlehotel.com. Luxury Victorian castle 3 miles (5km) northeast of Fort William on A82. Set in 50 acres (20 hectares) of woodland with splendid views of the loch and mountains. Fine cuisine, fishing, and boat trips on the loch. 17 rooms.

Kinloch Lodge ££££ *Sleat, Skye, IV43 8QY, tel: 01471-833333*, www.kinloch-lodge.co.uk. This is the home of the chief of Clan Macdonald and his wife, who is a notable cook and cookbook author. The manor has been expanded from a 1680 hunting lodge and contains family portraits and possessions. The wonderful food is based on traditional Scottish cuisine made with local ingredients. 15 rooms.

The Moorings Hotel ££ *Banavie, Fort William, PH33 7LY, tel: 01397-772797*, www.moorings-fortwilliam.co.uk. By the Caledonian Canal, the hotel has views of Ben Nevis. The pleasant bedrooms are nicely decorated. Award-winning restaurant. 27 rooms.

Scarista House £££ *Isle of Harris, Western Isles, HS3 3HX, tel: 01859-550238*, www.scaristahouse.com. This Georgian manse is set in a remote area overlooking a beach – perfect for getting away from it all. It has an outstanding restaurant. 6 rooms.

Summer Isles Hotel ££ *Achiltibuie, Ross-shire, IV26 2YG, tel: 01854-622282*, www.summerisleshotel.com. Open Easter–October. Over the years the hotel has established itself as an oasis of civilisation hidden away in a stunningly beautiful, but still wild and untouched landscape. Nearly everything you eat here is home produced or locally caught. 7 rooms, 2 suites and a cottage.

Tiroran House £££ *Mull, PA69 6ES (off the road to Iona on the B8035), tel: 01681-705232*, www.tiroran.com. This lovely country house is set in beautiful grounds with spacious lawns and gardens on the shore of Loch Scridain. Its public rooms and comfortable bedrooms are more like those in a home than a hotel. Good food is served in an elegant setting. Telephone for directions before you go or you'll run the risk of getting lost. 10 rooms plus self-catering cottages.

Western Isles Hotel ££ *Tobermory, Mull, PA75 6PR, tel: 01688-302012*, www.westernisleshotel.co.uk. A welcoming atmosphere greets the visitor to this traditional hotel that has spectacular views over the Sound of Mull and Tobermory Bay. The food is excellent and served in the formal dining room or charming conservatory. 26 rooms.

INDEX

Berlitz POCKET GUIDE

SCOTLAND

Fifth Edition 2016

Editor: Rachel Lawrence
Author: Alice Fellows
Updated by: Hilary Weston and Jackie Stadde
Head of Production: Rebeka Davies
Picture Editor: Tom Smyth
Cartography Update: Carte
Photography Credits: David Cruickshanks/
Apa Publications 4TL, 23, 29, 41, 47; Douglas
Macgilvray/Apa Publications 18; iStock 5MC,
21, 104; Mockford & Bonetti/Apa Publications
4MC, 4/5T, 6TL, 6TL, 6ML, 6ML, 6MC, 6/7M,
6/7M, 6/7T, 6/7T, 9, 9R, 15, 24, 26, 28, 31, 32,
33, 34, 35, 36, 37, 38, 39, 44, 45, 49, 51, 52, 57,
93, 94, 96; National Galleries of Scotland 20;
Public domain 17; Shutterstock 4ML, 5TC,
4/5M, 8, 48, 76, 78, 81, 82, 83
Cover Picture: 4Corners Images

Distribution
UK: Dorling Kindersley Ltd,
A Penguin Group company, 80 Strand, London
WC2R 0RL; sales@uk.dk.com
United States: Ingram Publisher Services,
1 Ingram Boulevard, PO Box 3006, La Vergne
TN 37086-1986; ips@ingramcontent.com
Australia and New Zealand: Woodslane,
10 Apollo St, Warriewood, NSW 2102,